WOMAN IN AMERICA;

BEING

AN EXAMINATION INTO

THE

MORAL AND INTELLECTUAL CONDITION

OF

AMERICAN FEMALE SOCIETY.

> Woman's empire is *Home*; and, by adding spirituality to its happiness, dignity to its dominion, and power to its influences, it becomes the best security for *individual integrity*, and the surest safeguard for *national virtue*.

BY MRS. A. J. GRAVES.

NEW-YORK:

HARPER AND BROTHERS, 82 CLIFF-ST

1843.

Entered, according to Act of Congress, in the year 1841, by
HARPER & BROTHERS,
In the Clerk's Office of the Southern District of New-York.

PREFACE.

The following work is not intended to be a manual of female duties; and, wherever these duties are mentioned, they are merely incidental to the subject. There are fundamental duties, of which no woman can plead ignorance, though many may plead incapacity as it regards their performance; but duty, in other respects, is a relative term, and belongs to the individual, not to the sex. It would, therefore, be no less unwise to form a fixed code of regulations to which every woman must conform, than to prescribe the same course of diet and regimen for the healthy man and the invalid.

Woman cannot complain of want of instruction; but the generality of her teachers content themselves with giving her certain tasks, without examining her mental or moral capabilities. They neglect the preliminary work, that of preparing the soil, in order that the seed so liberally cast abroad may germinate, spring up, and bear fruit. If women are taught to feel rightly, to think deeply, and to use their own powers in reaching an elevated standard of female character, they will be the most competent judges of their own duties, and best able to graduate for themselves the scale of their obligations.

All, therefore, that has been attempted in the following pages, is an examination into the present condition of American female society in its various classes—*not of station, but of character;* and in showing what American women are, the writer has endeavoured to stimulate them to become what they ought to be.

The plan and general features of the work were sketched several years ago, and have been gradually filled up at occasional moments of leisure; the importance of the truths recorded having been much more carefully attended to than the language or style in which they might appear. Although the sentiments it contains are the result of observation and reflection rather than of reading, yet, during its progress, several books have been consulted. In a few of these there was found a coincidence with some of the thoughts and opinions already written; but, wherever an after opportunity occurred for the expression of sentiments congenial to the known recorded sentiments of others, the writer has always preferred to give them as quotations instead of clothing them in her own language, and the names of the authors thus quoted are given in the course of the work.

The writer cannot conclude this preface without naming one book, which impressed her more deeply than any other she has ever read upon woman. This book is "Woman's Mission;" and although it was procured too late to bring its high authority in support of the opinions herein expressed as to the legitimate sphere and true social position of our sex, yet it was a cause of much gratification to find similar views so ably defended in that excellent work. Its condensed lessons of wisdom are more suited to thinkers than superficial readers; and this may prevent its being as universally popular as, from its great merits, it deserves. It is a book of texts, capable of being expanded into volumes of instruction; and it is one which every woman should study, deeply and prayerfully, that its principles may be exhibited in her life and conduct, and that her own appointed mission may be thoroughly understood and faithfully discharged.

CONTENTS.

Introduction . . . . Page 13

CHAPTER I.

DOMESTIC WOMEN.

Domestic Class still a numerous one.—Injurious Consequences arising from Prejudice against Labour.—Want of Preparation for Household Duties, its evil Effects upon Woman.—Trials of American Housekeepers.—Early Fading of American Women.—Waste of Female Labour.—Overtasked Strength.—Parents who make themselves Slaves to their Children.—Physical Education of Females even more important than that of Males.—Children of both Sexes should be encouraged in active Sports.—Duty of Mothers in regard to Physical Training . . . . Page 23

CHAPTER II.

DOMESTIC WOMEN—CONTINUED.

Domestic Employments the best Exercise for Females.—Indolent Habits fatal to the Interests of the Sex.—The Value of a well-ordered Home.—Are such Homes increasing?—Causes of their Decrease.—Responsibility of Woman in making Home what it should be.—Woman's Influence in promoting the Intellectual and Moral Elevation of the Family.—The Patriotism of Woman not to be exhibited in Political Partisanship.—Dignity of Domestic Duties when rightly considered.—

Evils of helpless Dependance on Servants.—Can they be dispensed with?—Opinion of Dr. Alcott on this Subject.—Increased Number of Servants employed in Families.—Servants a neglected Class.—Ignorance and Inefficiency in the House-keeper.—Want of proper Works on Domestic Economy.—Woman herself the best Teacher . . . . Page 50

CHAPTER III.

FASHIONABLE WOMEN.

The Fashionable Class: their Characteristics.—Both Sexes Slaves to Fashion.—Injurious Effects of Fashionable Extravagance upon Individual and National Character.—Few Examples of Republican Simplicity.—The Passion for Extravagance a National Trait.—Evidences of Female Extravagance as shown by our Imports.—The general Love of Finery.—Sedgwick. — Folly of extravagant Entertainments. — How Evening Parties might be made beneficial to both Sexes.—Erroneous Female Education the Cause of the general Passion for what is frivolous, and the Indifference to what is great.—Defective Systems of Female Training in Childhood and in more advanced Years.—Fashionable Schools anti-domestic.—Predilection for Boarding instead of Housekeeping.—Woman educated for the World.—Importance of correct Female Education 93

CHAPTER IV.

RELIGIOUS WOMEN.

Religious Class comparatively large.—Its Influence.—Female Co-operation in the Public Duties of Religion and Benevolence.—Its Tendency to draw Woman from Home.—She is not alone to be blamed.—Woman intended to be a Keeper at Home.—Scripture Doctrine of Parental Responsibility.—Parents should maintain the Honour of the Family Institution, and carefully watch all that is anti-domestic in the Movements of the Day.—Characteristics of the Age.—Influence of the Spirit of the Age upon the Female Sex.—Importance of the Domestic Circle.—Woman's true Mission.—Woman should exert a counterbalancing Influence against the Excitements of the Age.—These Excitements increasing, and the Family Institution declining.—Woman's Duty in making this Institution what God designed it should be.—Some Tokens of better Things to come.—Materual Associations.—Happy Influences to be exercised by Christian Homes upon Individuals and upon the Nation . . . . . . Page 137

CHAPTER V.

INTELLECTUAL WOMEN.

Intellectual Women of our Country more indebted to Self-training than to our Systems of Education.—Women of extensive Acquirements.—The Intellectual Class.—Advancement of the general Female Mind.—The Controversy concerning the Intellectual Equality of the Sexes vain and unprofitable.—Impossibility of satisfactorily deciding the Question.—Ulterior Objects of the Discussion.—Political Rights of Woman examined.—Dangers of Ultraism.—The True Rights of Woman in Danger of being lost sight of in defending or opposing those which are imaginary.—Doctrine of Human Rights.—Inalienable Rights derived from God; Social and Political Rights from the Institutions of Man.—The Husband and the Wife.—Civil Authority given to Man; Influence over the Mind and Morals to Woman.—The Real Wrongs of the Sex a sufficient Field for all the Exertions of Female Reformers.—Errors of such Reformers in looking to Female Representation and Legislation for the Establishment of Woman's Rights.—Enlightened Public Opinion the only thing to be relied on.—The Importance of Female Education not yet understood.—No available Progress has been made, if American Women are not qualified to educate the future Men of our Country.—Intellectual Acquirements merely the Means to an End: instance, the Art of Reading.—The general Mind of Society to be estimated by its Literature.—This Test applied to the Aggregate Intellectual Character of American Women.—Female Reading.—Novels.—Female Periodicals.—Three Exceptions to their general Character.—Signs of better Things.—Want of a National Literature.—The Necessity of having one.—Duty of American Female Writers.—The best Models for the Exercise of their Genius.—All Women who are capable should unite in elevating the Intellectual Condition of their Sex . . . . Page 164

CHAPTER VI.

WOMEN WHO ARE MORALLY GREAT.

Moral Greatness a rare Attainment.—Edinburgh Review.—Examples of Female Moral Greatness in English History.—Mrs. Hutchinson.—Lady Russel.—Madame Roland contrasted with Madame de Staël.—Character of Madame Roland.—Few Examples of Female Moral Greatness recorded in American History.—The Women of the Revolution.—Mother of Washington.—Existing Circumstances unfavourable to Female Moral Greatness.—Want of Responsibility.—False Views of the Position of Woman.—Their injurious Effects upon both Sexes.—The beneficial Effects of Self-dependance shown by Examples from real Life.—Moral Strength to Woman a difficult Attainment—Native Force of Character insufficient.—Genius equally powerless.—Examples.—Mrs. Hemans and Miss Landon.—Moral Strength in Woman must be cultivated.—Its Necessity.—Duty of Parents.—Duty of Husbands.—Woman wronged by injudicious Training.—By being Censured for Faults the Result of such Training.—Woman's Duty to herself and to her Sex, in giving energy to the Female Character.—Christianity the only True Foundation of Female Moral Greatness 196

Conclusion 254

INTRODUCTION.

The present age is in many respects a remarkable—a wonderful one: it is the age of moral revolutions. Throughout the whole civilized world we see conflicting elements convulsing and agitating the different masses of society, and out of this seemingly chaotic confusion, the philanthropist, the patriot, and the Christian hope to see gradually evolved beautiful systems of harmony, order, and just proportion. The fountains of the great deep seem broken up. The roaring and dashing waters of the deluge of human opinions have not yet subsided into their appointed place, nor has the dove of promise yet brought its olive-branch to make known to us that the reign of peace and safety is restored to the earth.

The great principles of liberty and equal rights, which are about to overthrow the long-existing institutions of despotism, and are stirring the hearts of men of every station, in every clime, have penetrated even into the quiet havens of domestic life. While men are fiercely contending for their prerogatives upon the world's arena, without seeming yet to have settled what should be their relative position in regard to each other, women have come forward to claim immunities which ancient usage has long denied them. "The Rights of Woman" are almost as warmly and wildly contested as "The Rights of Man;" and there is a revolution going on in the female mind at the present day, out of which glorious results may arise; though in this, as in all other revolutions, ultraism and fanaticism may retard the development of good by their excesses, and their disregard of the dictates of sound wisdom and sober discretion. We lament the erratic course of many of our female reformers, believing that they have inflicted deep injury where they intended good, by drawing woman away from her true and allotted sphere—domestic life. Nor are our female lecturers and female politicians alone at fault; for it is to be feared that even some Christian ministers, with greater zeal than knowledge, have, by their impassioned appeals, sent woman abroad into the highways and by-ways of life, thereby deadening their sense of home responsibilities and social duties, and teaching them to violate that Gospel injunction which plainly declares that women should be "keepers at home." And painful is it to every well-wisher of our sex, and to all who would see it elevated to its proper station, to see talents and energies wasted in feeble and fruitless efforts to tranquillize and clear the stormy and turbid waters of public life, which might be so usefully and effectually employed in purifying each fountain-head in the sequestered vales of home, that they would send forth living and refreshing streams to fertilize and make beautiful the moral wilderness of the world.

In the revolutions going on in society, the female sex is doubtless destined to act a most important part, and to rise to a station far beyond that which she has at present attained. There are capabilities in woman that have never been developed. She has not fulfilled her destined mission, nor is she as yet prepared to fulfil it. Much remains to be done before she can occupy that position in society for which she was created, and given to man. The pernicious effects of the slavery to which she was subjected in past ages of heathenism and ignorance still cling to her, nor has she learned to appreciate and improve, as she ought, the precious boon of liberty Christianity has extended to her. Woman must learn to respect herself, and to *merit* that respect from man which is her due; nor will she ever be thoroughly emancipated until her education from the cradle to the grave is far different from what it ever has been. The errors, weaknesses, and foibles instilled into her infancy, are in her womanhood strengthened by intercourse with society, and by the circumstances in which she is placed. She is yet too often found either the petted, capricious plaything, or the toiling, careworn slave; and thus she lives and dies, without knowing or fulfilling her responsibilities as the helpmate of her brother man—a being intended to be a co-worker with him in promoting the spiritual and intellectual advancement of the race. It is true there are bright examples here and there of women whose blessed influence sheds a halo around them; but of the mass this sketch is not too darkly drawn, for it is delineated from real life, and the broad field of long-continued observation.

But there is evidently a change gradually taking place in the female sex which gives promise of better things to come. The subject of female influence, as an instrument of *great moral power*, is attracting earnest attention in every part of Christendom. In Europe as well as America, the efforts made to elevate the female mind, though they have been the occasion of some extravagances, may yet eventuate in its moral and intellectual advancement. Philosophers, statesmen, and Christian philanthropists have begun to speculate, write, and preach on woman's influence, and on her importance as an educator of the rising generation. Nor have their appeals been made in vain. Woman has taken up the work of her own social regeneration. The women of France, of England, and of America seem to be wakening to a sense of the responsibilities devolving on their sex, and are beginning to put forth their exertions in the great cause of female improvement. Although there are traits common to woman in all climes, yet she everywhere possesses, equally with man, a distinctive national character. Hence we see the same spirit of reform taking, in some respects, a different direction in different countries; for it is evident that a reformation attempted in any community should be suited to its particular wants, capacities, and social institutions.

That the general character of American women has been modified by the circumstances which have formed that of our men, seems to be sufficiently apparent; and, among other evidences, from the concurrent testimony of foreign travellers. By some of these we have been censured, and by others commended, according to their peculiar views, or the strength of their national prejudices; but in this they all agree. The thinking De Tocqueville, in speaking of our country, says: "I have nowhere seen women occupying a loftier position (that is, of moral influence);" and he does not hesitate to ascribe our "singular and growing strength as a people" to the superiority of our women. What superiority we may possess in comparison with the females of other countries, we know not; but it must be evident to every American woman who is anxious to see her sex occupying the lofty position it might, that we are far from being all that American women should be. Under a government like ours, the responsibility of woman becomes tenfold greater than in the monarchies of Europe. In every country, the formation of the character of the rising generation is doubtless a subject of deep interest, from the moral influence it must exert; but where, as in ours, the government is vested in the people, it becomes also an object of the highest political importance. Every mother in our land may have under her forming care its future rulers and statesmen; and in every son she is intrusted with a being who, if he live to manhood, will exercise a voice in the promotion of measures to operate either for his country's weal or wo. It is for her, then, to form good citizens as well as good men. To make *partizan politicians* is no part of her duty; but to form sound, thinking minds, capable of rightly exercising their future privileges as freemen; and virtuous characters, whose influence will be exerted in the cause of truth, wisdom, and righteousness. What, then, we may ask, is the actual state of American female society? To what degree are the aggregate character and intellect of our women fitted for the performance of their social responsibilities? and how far are our manners and habits such as become the daughters of our free Republic?

In glancing our eye over the broad surface of American female society, amid the endless varieties of individual character, we still see enough of similarity, in regard to certain prominent features, to arrange it into separate classes. But these classes are not graduated by the outward circumstances of birth, station, or wealth; for it is apparent to every observer of human nature, that the vulgar and unintellectual woman of wealth and high standing in conventional life, is essentially the same as the one of like mind occupying a more humble position in society. The hired servant, or the tradesman's wife, whose whole pleasure consists in display and personal decoration, and who expends her money upon frippery to the full extent of her slender finances, is intrinsically in no degree inferior to the wife of the wealthy merchant or banker, whose ostentatious extravagance of living is fostered by a liberal allowance from her husband's funds, or indulged upon the false basis of his inflated credit. Our high places are open to all who strive to reach them; and, therefore, the only classification that our institutions will warrant, is that which is based upon character, and not upon the accidents of rank or fortune. An English female writer says, that "in no other country is society so beautifully proportioned" as in her own; where the national column finds its base " in the laborious poor, its pillar in the middle classes, and its rich and highly-ornamented capital in the ancient nobility of the land." This order is of man's designing; but ours—a more noble and enduring one—an equality of rights and privileges—was founded by the Creator of the universe himself; and the similitude of our glorious institutions is found in the lofty mountain, whose heights are free to all who are able to scale them; and over whose summit our own eagle expands his wings, protecting all, and allowing peculiar favours to none.

Although, in making a classification of our females, there may be some "bright, particular stars" who do not seem to come within the orbit of any one described; and though there may be others, again, who possess qualities belonging to different ones, yet, on the whole, the several classes may be designated with sufficient accuracy to suit our purpose. There are other modifications, also, produced by local circumstances in different parts of our widely-extended country. Thus the women of the Eastern States, those of the South, and the wives and daughters of the great West, have each their distinctive peculiarities; and should either of these portions be unfairly represented in classifying the women of America, the error must be pardoned, as resulting from want of sufficient information, and not from intention.

If the improvement of females, and the importance of their receiving a more thorough and judicious education, for time and for eternity, than has hitherto been given them, be a prominent object to which the attention of *man* is being earnestly directed, how much more deeply must this subject be impressed on the heart of every woman who is the friend and well-wisher of her sex? The prevailing defects of females are more generally the result of their training than of their nature; and the author trusts that in pointing them out she will not be deemed censorious, for she is deeply sensible of her own failings and incapabilities in common with others. In the words of Miss Hannah More, she possesses " that lively interest which can only flow from the tender and intimate participation of fellow-feeling. And surely an earnest wish to turn their attention to objects calculated to promote their true dignity is not the office of an enemy. So to expose the weakness of the land as to suggest the necessity of internal improvement, and to point out the means of effectual defence, is not treachery, but patriotism."

WOMAN IN AMERICA.

CHAPTER I.

DOMESTIC WOMEN.

"The duties and destinies of the housekeeper are too important to be misunderstood. The elements of the nation, nay, of the world itself, are prepared, to a very great extent, in our nurseries and around the domestic fireside."—DR. ALCOTT.

THOUGH the spirit of the present age is in many respects unfavourable to the cultivation of the household virtues, yet by far the largest portion of our females may be included in the domestic class. Many are "keepers at home" from inclination, some from a sense of duty, and others from the force of necessity. Of these, some are essentially domestic in their habits and tastes from childhood to womanhood; and a great number, who have once been devoted to the gayeties of society, have found, upon becoming wives and mothers, that enough of the woman was still left alive in their hearts to make the pleasures of home more attractive than any that the world could offer. The difficulty of procuring well-trained servants, or any assistant sufficiently faithful to fill her place, as the regulator and manager of the household, keeps also many a woman 'in her station, who would otherwise be very willing to transfer most of her responsibilities and duties to any substitute who should be deemed capable of discharging them. And it is well, perhaps, that this necessity operates so universally; for, from whatever cause her keeping at home may arise, the effect is, no doubt, of incalculable benefit to herself, to her husband, and to her children.

For a woman to be domestic is so consonant with every feeling of her heart, and so true to her nature, that where she is not so it must be the result of a training which has counteracted the designs of Providence, and guided her contrary to her innate propensities; and wherever we find her removed from the corrupt influences of fashion and of an erroneous education, we there see her the light of her home, the guide of her household, and the active and efficient helpmate of her husband. It is a subject of heart-cheering gratulation, that in our land such women are " not a few;" and though the domestic class is rapidly decreasing in numbers before the flood of European follies pouring in upon us, and from the false opinions respecting woman's duties and privileges so extensively circulated, yet we rest our hopes upon the glorious remnant who have not yet bowed the knee to foreign usages, whose minds have not been unsettled from their true faith, and who have never been found wandering from their proper sphere at the call of disorganizing fanatics, whether political, philosophical, or religious. To this phalanx we look for aid in arresting the march of error wherever it is seen advancing, whether it be in habits or manners, in doctrines or in morals.

Among the many causes that are tending to deaden in the heart of woman a sense of her appropriate obligations, is the fatal notion that there is something servile in labour. It is, indeed, much to be lamented, that in the praiseworthy effort to redeem herself from the life of slavery and degradation to which past ages doomed her, so many of her sex should have passed to the other extreme—a life of indolence and uselessness. Nor is this notion, that there is gentility in idleness, confined to females alone: we find it widely and deeply cherished by society at large. Hence we see that the aristocratic titles of "lady" and "gentleman" are by common consent thought to be applicable only to those who hold it beneath their fancied dignity to toil with their hands. The farmer who guides his own plough, and the mechanic who still plies his tools, are thus considered as belonging to a lower caste than the "gentleman" farmer who lives solely upon the toil of his dependant labourers, or the retired mechanic who has thrown aside his implements, and employs the capital amassed by their use in extensive speculations in lands or stocks.

This idea of the servility of labour, transmitted to us from the feudal prejudices of Europe, has wrought much greater evil in our republican country than in the nations from which we have servilely received it. It is not indigenous to our institutions, either political or social, though the poisonous exotic has flourished luxuriantly throughout our land and in our homes. It has, to a great extent, made our men anxious, slavish worshippers of Mammon, and a large proportion of our women idle lovers of pleasure; whose god is vanity, and whose ruling passion is a craving for the "lust of the eyes and the pride of life." For it is not avarice that crowds our cities with those who are "making haste to be rich;" it is the desire to be lifted above the necessity of labour, and to secure the luxury of indolent leisure. Nor is it natural listlessness that fills our houses with those useless incumbrances, *fine ladies;* it is the false idea that domestic employments are employments to be ashamed of, and altogether unsuited to the dignity of "a lady."

Strange is it, that in this age, considered so intellectual, and in this country, so often boasted of as the most enlightened among nations, that manual labour should be looked upon as a degradation. The pernicious effects of this prejudice are seen on every side, and in both sexes; and its consequences are as fatal to individual well-being as to our national prosperity. The mass of young men pressing forward into professional or mercantile life, with scarcely a prospect of success from over-competition, look down with disdain upon the pursuits of the practical agriculturist or of the mechanic, whose industry rarely fails to secure its reward. And many of our females, in their ambition to be considered "ladies," refuse to aid their toiling mothers, lest their fair hands should lose their softness and delicacy, and, while using these useless appendages in playing with their ringlets, or touching the piano or guitar, they will speak with contempt of the household drudge, and boast of their "lady-like" ignorance of domestic employments. But women who thus spend their days in idleness and folly, are by far more deserving of contempt than she whose time and thoughts are wholly occupied in the necessary manual labours of her nursery and her kitchen, and who knows nothing beyond them. It is true, she may be, as a late writer remarks, as unfit a companion for a man of sense and education as the "lowest servant" could be; but still she fulfils her part to the utmost extent of her capacity, and in providing a comfortable and well-ordered home for her husband and children, "she hath done what she could," and will reap her reward. And in the present state of society, where the opinion is still so current, even among men of intellect, that a wife was intended to be nothing higher than the obsequious ministering servant of man—a menial without wages—such a one is, and ever ought to be, more valued as a companion for life, than she who is ignorant of domestic duties, and skilled only in mere accomplishments, and in the art of decorating her person.

A woman who is incapable of intellectual enjoyments, and whose mind and feelings are centred in her household employments, and aspire no higher, finds no drudgery in her labours. If physically fitted to perform them, and fully prepared for them by knowledge and practice, they are to her a source of positive happiness. "She worketh willingly with her hands, she looketh well to the ways of her household, and eateth not the bread of idleness." Like the industrious bee, the hum of cheerful activity is heard in her home from early dawn to the evening hour; and the frown of discontent, and the listlessness of ennui, are never seen to cloud her placid brow. But, though a life of laborious occupation may thus be made one of happiness as well as usefulness, yet woman was placed in this world to fill a station embracing far higher duties than those of a mere domestic labourer. She has been endowed with intellectual faculties and moral influence, which were designed to be cultivated, not only for her own advancement, but to fit her to be the educator of her children and the improver of her husband, when called upon to discharge these important social obligations. The true sphere of a wife and mother is not that merely of a ministering servant to the physical wants and necessities of her family; it is to be the enlightened instructer and guide of awakening minds, her husband's counsellor, the guardian and purifier of the morals of her household.

The term "domestic drudge" is unfitly applied to that woman to whom active labour is rendered delightful by sound health and long experience in household employments, even though her want of mental cultivation should incapacitate her for her higher responsibilities: it would appear to be more appropriate to that female who knows these employments are her duties, and also anxiously strives to perform them, under a keen sense of physical inability; and the energies of whose spirit are broken down in the hopeless attempt to discharge her obligations, with the disadvantages which a want of previous training has inflicted upon her. Nor is it only those who become wives after having spent their girlhood in folly and indolence, that are deficient in the knowledge of household affairs; for many a woman of intellect, on becoming a housekeeper, finds herself equally unprepared for the station she has assumed. Her devotion to books, and her sedentary habits, have produced a morbid refinement of tastes, an indisposition to active employments, and a consequent debility of body, which unfit her for domestic duties. She may have even, before her marriage, thought and read so much on household economy as to be deeply impressed with its importance, and formed from her own reflection a beautiful theory, whose practice was to be found easy and delightful; and yet, when it comes to be tested by application, she is overwhelmed by unexpected difficulties. The model formed in her mind was intended to move readily and harmoniously; but she finds its machinery, in all its parts, so impeded by friction as to be wholly unfit for its destined purpose. She has looked only on the great result — a well-ordered home — without having had any idea of the minute and perplexing details necessary to its attainment.

Her imaginary scheme was based on her presumed ability to perform her part as the governing and directing power, and in the expectation of having well-trained and efficient operatives to fulfil theirs; and in both of these she is bitterly disappointed. Want of practical knowledge, and the unskilfulness of inexperience, cause what little strength she possesses to be ineffectually expended, and she is awakened to a mortifying consciousness of her deficiencies. Her servants are not only " given to eye-service," but are careless, faithless, and inefficient, and often ignorant of the very duties they were hired to perform, expecting to be taught how

to do, instead of being simply ordered to do
It is not always at her command to say to one,
Go, and she goeth; and to another, Come, and
she cometh; for, instead of this willing obedience, she will often meet with open impertinence or ill-suppressed murmurings, even when
requiring a reasonable service, and one that
they themselves must know is " nominated in
the bond."

To have her work done as it should be, she
finds that she needs the quick, observing glance;
an Argus power of vision, and almost the gift
of ubiquity; for she is considered responsible
not only for what has been done, but for what
is *being* done. If, from restricted circumstances, she is obliged to take upon herself so
much of the labour of some one of her domestic employments as to confine her to a particular department of duty, to the consequent neglect of a constant inspection of the whole, it
is then that she feels the full bitterness of her
wearisome life. Like the toiling Sisyphus, her
years are spent in labours which to her show
no satisfying result. The physical wants of
her family demand so much of her time, that
she is unable to fulfil, as faithfully as her conscience urges her to do, the higher duties she
owes them; and it is then, in the eloquent lan-

guage of Mrs. Gilman, that " cares eat away her heart; the day presses on her with new toils; the night comes, and they are unfulfilled; she lies down in weariness, and rises with uncertainty; her smiles become languid and few, and her husband wonders at the gloominess of his home."

This may appear an exaggerated picture to such as relinquish the care of their families to their servants, or to those fortunate females who, by a judicious, early training in domestic duties, have found the management of their household a pleasant and easy occupation; but the force of its truth will be felt by many a woman, and its original may be found in many a home throughout our land. There are numerous bitter trials peculiar to the American housekeeper, which, from a better regulated system of household service, are unknown to the women of Europe. Though, as Mrs. Sigourney justly observes, " the difficulty of procuring well-trained servants is a tax which all should be willing to pay for the privilege of our government," yet it is one which bears heavily on the females of the United States, where so few are found independent enough to adopt a mode of living strictly in accordance with the republican simplicity of our institutions. " It is worthy of remark," says Mrs. Farrar, " that in this country, where it is so difficult to procure a sufficiency of household labour, the mode of furnishing a house and conducting the business of a family is such as to require more attendance than the same style of living would demand in France and other parts of Europe." And if such be the opinion of a daughter of New-England, where, from the long-experienced scarcity of servants, girls are early trained to active usefulness, and where more attention is paid to the economy of labour in household affairs, how much more forcibly will it apply to those states in which the habits of females are still suffering from the effects of having been accustomed, not many years back, to slave attendants, and where, at present, the sole dependance in domestic service is upon hired assistants, so often capricious in their character and inefficient in their stations? In the slave states, where the housekeeper has for her servants those whom she claims as her property, and most of whom have been born and brought up in her own family or in that of her parents, the affairs of the household are generally conducted with more regularity and order than they possibly can be where there is a continual change of domestics, unless, indeed, the wife and mother be also her own "maid of all work." The mistress of a retinue of slaves is by no means devoid of trials, but then they are different in many respects from those experienced by her who is wholly dependant upon hired labour.

Our women are generally less fitted for active household duties than in some countries are those even of the higher classes, who are never placed under the necessity of performing them. The extreme fragility and early fading of American females have been ascribed to early marriages; and this, doubtless, may contribute to such an effect; but the most extensively operating cause is to be found in the almost total neglect of active exercise, either in the house or in the open air, added to a want of prudent adaptation of clothing to the vicissitudes of our climate. Instead of the robust forms and the rosy hue of health so common among females even in the circles of European nobility, where a proper physical education is better understood and practised, we find, with us, groups of pale and delicate women entering upon the trying duties of wives, mothers, and housekeepers, wholly unprepared and unfitted for them; and need we wonder that so many of them so soon break, and droop, and die in early womanhood? Here, in our cities at least, it is comparatively rare to see an aged couple who have " clam the hill of life thegither." Let every woman pause, and call to mind the many young and lovely married and unmarried females, who have fallen around her into an untimely grave, and she will then feel the necessity of doing her part in arousing her sex to a sense of the present and future evils of their suicidal course of life.

The great amount and waste of female labour and energy required in our households, with our present style of living; the inefficiency and incapacity of those from whom this labour is required, and the difficulty of procuring aid in lightening it, produce a fearful aggregate of ills, and a degree of suffering both physical and mental, which woman alone can appreciate and feel. The life-consuming trials of many a domestic history might be unfolded, which to man would appear incredible; and even by the husbands who witnessed them would neither be felt nor understood, from their ignorance of the peculiar nature of woman's feelings and susceptibilities. These household trials fall most heavily upon those women who, striving to maintain their station in fashionable society, are forced by limited means to become their own housekeepers, in order to unite the strictest economy in their internal regulations with an outward show before the world. The efforts required to keep up appearances in regard to their families and domestic establishments, and the mortifying consciousness that their servants are witnesses of the many mean and petty shifts to which they are obliged to resort, must be galling in the extreme to their worldly pride. And when we reflect upon "the wear and tear" of their energies, from the midnight toils undergone for the sake of securing the gentility of leisure at the hours of the fashionable morning call; the slavish fear of being surprised in some menial employment; the efforts in rallying their jaded spirits before their visiters; the incessant requisitions upon their time from their husbands and children, added to the weariness and exhaustion of an overtasked frame, while demands for repose must be sternly denied—when we think of these things, we cannot be surprised that so many women become doubly martyrs, by making themselves the slaves of this unnatural union of domestic labours with fashionable folly.

The evils resulting from overtasked strength are often as fatal to the disposition and character as to health and life. The constant irritation produced by heedless servants, and the painful consciousness of having more to attend to than there is capability or time to accomplish, produce that fretful impatience and peevish discontent so frequently observable in the careworn mistresses of large families. The exhaustion of body, and the languor and weariness consequent upon over-exertion, not unfrequently bring on a craving for artificial stimulants, especially when the thought of labours still to be performed forbids the rest that nature requires. Any excessive or too long-continued exercise, either of the mental or physical powers, has a debilitating effect upon the body; and hence we find the hard student and the overworked labourer equally exposed to the temptation of seeking a temporary capability for farther efforts from the injurious excitement of the various kinds of stimulants, instead of renovating their natural strength by judiciously abstaining from their toils. None suffer more from this languor and weariness than the delicate female, whose duties call for unremitting bodily exertion and constant vigilance of mind; and thus so many of our sex resort to the strong cup of tea or coffee, while others substitute the glass of wine, the small dose of opium, and sometimes even the sweetened mixture of stronger draughts, with the erroneous idea of recovering by these means that strength which can be healthfully restored only by quiet and repose. The transient excitement thus produced is quickly followed by a reaction, which not only leaves them still more feeble than before, but creates the necessity of gradually increasing the power of the stimulant, that it may produce the desired effect. Many women have suffered deeply in their health and energies by such a course, though regard for their husband and children, and for their own character, may have prevented them from giving way to the daily and habitual use of stimulants. But there are some who have continued to advance unconsciously in their ruinous career, until they have become worse than lost to their families and friends, in the fiery gulf of intemperance. I have heard two or three histories of real life, sketches of which would be more appalling than the most vividly-drawn tale in our temperance annals: instances where woman, lovely, educated woman, from having been the idol of fashionable life and the delight of her home, became so debased a thing as to be an outcast from society, and the jest and scorn of her lowest menial.

Since, then, so many of the trials which break down the spirit of woman in domestic life are occasioned by a want of preparation for its duties; and so much of the debility, suffering, and disease that fall to her lot, exposing her to the temptation of seeking their alleviation in ruinous expedients, may be ascribed to the neglect of physical education, how imperative is the demand upon every mother throughout our land to train up her daughters to industry, activity, and usefulness. The erroneous maxim so often repeated, that "girls should *enjoy* themselves while single, because, poor things, they will have *trouble enough* when they are married," is as false in principle as in the terms used to express it. *True enjoyment* is never found in indolence or in dissipating amusements; and the *trouble* of married life is chiefly occasioned by those very habits which are supposed to constitute the enjoyment of girlhood. "I do not know how some of my acquaintance find time to do their own sewing," said a young lady, with much self-complacency; "mine is wholly taken up in dressing myself, paying morning calls, and sitting on the sofa to receive my visiters." I could not help sighing when I thought what a poor prospect for happiness she had before her;

for she was not averse to the attentions of gentlemen, and no doubt expected to be married. She had neither the beauty, fortune, nor accomplishments which could lead her to hope for what is called a "great match"—one that would seem to ensure a life without labour—and this was her preparation for future duties! Can we wonder that such a one should become a useless encumbrance—a drawback, instead of being a helpmate to her husband, and a neglectful and inefficient mother of children? In despite of her frequent gayety and animation, the incipient *malade imaginaire* was shadowed forth in her affected languor, and in her inclination to exaggerate every trifling indisposition, the growing results of want of exercise and of active employment. Would that the united experience of every husband and wife among us could be related in the hearing, and impressed upon the heart of every mother in our land, that she might feel, and deeply feel, this truth: that wherever peace and love nestle in quiet happiness around the domestic hearth, they have been for the most part attracted there by industry and health; and that, where discontent, irritability of temper, and estrangement of affection are found among the inmates of home, they may be ascribed chiefly to the absence of the domestic virtues, and of habits of usefulness in the wife, which should have been assiduously cultivated under the parental roof.

Many mothers and daughters rest in the hope that the household virtues will come of themselves when they are called for; but a sad disappointment will break upon them when it is too late to repair the fatal error. It is true, we occasionally see women who, by the force of a good constitution, and great native energy of character, are enabled to overcome the evils of former neglect; but these cases are too rare to afford any ground of reasonable reliance. It is strange that experience should not have taught mothers a better lesson; that they do not universally feel the necessity of training their daughters aright, as well for their own comfort, as for the future happiness and well-being of their offspring. And yet we see mothers toiling on from day to day; overwhelmed with the pressure of domestic cares; wearing out their life, and shortening its natural period by exertions to which their age and failing strength are wholly inadequate; and who still permit their daughters to waste their hours in idleness or in trifling occupations, and neglect to call upon them for that assistance they so much need. The mother who thus makes herself a slave to her family is as unjust to her children as she is to herself; and the pain and suffering she endures will, by her means, be visited upon those whom, in her ill-judging tenderness, she is indulging in habits of indolence and uselessness. As soon as children are of sufficient age to minister to the wants of their parents, they should be required to do so. These services should always be proportioned to their years and their strength; but when time has at length brought their powers to maturity, the father and mother should then retire from laborious duty to the undisturbed quiet and repose of their firesides, and leave their sons to provide for their necessities, and their daughters to take upon themselves the burden of household management. But how seldom do we find this realized? In place of it, we often see aged fathers, whose few remaining locks are whitened by the many years that have passed over them, still treading with trembling steps the same fatiguing round of business duties, while their sons are, perhaps, rioting in dissipation, or living in indolence, on the means thus painfully accumulated; and many, many a toil-spent, "time-worn mother," too, still "hastening with anxious solicitude to answer every call from every member of the family, as if her part in the duties of life was not only to have waited upon her children in infancy, but to conduct them to an easy and luxurious old age; in short, to spare their feet from walking, their hands from labour, and their heads from thought." How frequently, also, do we see grown-up daughters not only permitting their mothers to wait upon them, but requiring their attendance, and often thanklessly receiving their services, or requiting them with expressions of irritation and peevishness, and sometimes of derision or contempt!! But even should this be the lamentable result of the mother's improper training, and in it she is only reaping the bitter fruits of her own planting, still it is no excuse for them: they should remember, that from excess of kindness alone, however much mistaken, she has made herself their slave, and that they, of all others, should be the last to visit upon her the sad effects of her error.

Often, too, we find girls naturally kind-hearted and well-meaning, who, from having been constantly accustomed to depend upon their mother to supply all their wants, and seeing her wholly devoted to the cares of her family, never once reflect on their own responsibilities, and that it is their place to render attentions instead of receiving them, and to take upon themselves the duties they thoughtlessly leave their parent. Many thus sin against the dictates of natural affection, unintentionally, because unreflectingly; but this should not be; for every daughter ought to study how she may best make some suitable return for the watchful care that nurtured her from helpless infancy to years of womanhood. It is a fatal mistake in parents to continue, throughout their lives, to be the ministering servants of their offspring. Fathers should be the patriarchal sovereigns, and mothers the queens of their households; and every child should be so trained as to yield them the willing homage of attention and respect no less than of affection. And they who abdicate the throne legitimately belonging to them either through neglect or weak indulgence, will find, in their old age, that there will be none to rise up and " do them reverence."

We see, then, that mothers, for their own sakes as well as their children's, should give earnest heed that their daughters be brought up " in the way they should go." If they wish to have their old age made one of ease and comfort; if they desire to see their daughters healthy, happy, and useful, cheerfully fulfilling the duties devolving upon them under the parental roof, or becoming the delight of a well-ordered home of their own, then let them remember that such blessings can be attained only by an early initiation into a judicious course of active domestic employments.

It was a remark of the late Dr. Spurzheim, that "the physical education of women was of more importance to the welfare of the world than that of men." The truth of this declaration is evident from observation, as well as the slightest acquaintance with the laws of physiology; and even if some be disposed to question whether it is *more* important to one sex than the other, yet all must acknowledge that there is a greater necessity for teaching its principles to females, from their almost universal neglect of them. Boys need but little training on this subject; for they accomplish their own physical training from earliest childhood, by active sports in the house and on the playground. The hammer and the saw are soon wielded by the little hand with a force apparently disproportioned to its size, and riding on the stick in boisterous merriment is continued to a length of time that would weary the strength of an adult. It is by amusements like these that boys overcome the evil effects of confinement to the limits of the nursery; but when the captives come to be liberated from their prison, and permitted to have free access to the fresh air of the fields and the woods, they need no instruction or stimulus to induce them to work out their own proper physical education.

With girls, however, it is quite different: their natural disposition leads them to less active pastimes; and this disposition is carefully strengthened by the oft-repeated admonition that they should not romp nor make a noise, and that active spirits will make them rude and unlady-like. But, though their natural taste furnishes an indication that their constitutions do not require that they should mingle in those boyish amusements which demand more muscular energy than they possess, yet they should be encouraged heartily to engage in such active and innocent plays as they can take pleasure in, instead of being checked and restrained whenever they are disposed to indulge in them. Girls very early show a wish to imitate in their amusements the various kinds of household occupation; and the little broom and duster, and the tiny washing-tub and smoothing-iron, are generally their favourite playthings. They find a happiness in waiting and tending, and in thinking they can be of use; and instead of teaching them the fatal error that it is servants, and not young ladies, who should do these things, let them be permitted to assist, even where their assistance tends more to interrupt than to aid; for the inculcation of habits of activity and usefulness is of far more importance than the loss of time incurred in rectifying their little mistakes. Nor should the fresh air, which enlivens the spirits of their brothers, and mantles their cheeks with the rosy hue of health, be denied to their sisters. Let these, too, have their garden-plot and their little hoe; and give them likewise the freedom of the meadows, of the hills and woodlands, where they will find amusements suited to their age and sex, in gathering wild-flowers to decorate their mother's mantel, or in transplanting them into their little flower-beds.

Let mothers bear in mind, then, that the active sports of boys, and the busy pastimes of girls, however annoying they may be, are as real indications of natural wants as hunger or thirst; and that it is as cruel and hurtful to deny them these, as to refuse them food to eat or water to drink. No child can be forced to sit still for an hour or two against its inclination, without suffering injury both mental and physical; and though in cases of sickness it may be necessary to keep them quiet, yet let not this be done when no such necessity exists. Occasional restraints at such times may be made useful lessons of self-control, by an appeal to their affection or benevolence, thus inducing them to sacrifice their own pleasures to the comfort of another; but never let the motive of this unnatural restraint upon the activity of childhood arise, as is too often the case, solely from parental selfishness.

It is a duty incumbent upon every mother to study the principles of physiology and dietetics, so far as they relate to the physical education of children. But to attempt in this place to give lessons on these subjects, would only be to quote the teachings of others, better qualified by their superior knowledge for that office, and whose works are within the reach of every one disposed to seek such information. I shall confine my remarks, therefore, to the importance of domestic employments, as one of the means of health, usefulness, and happiness.

E

CHAPTER II.

DOMESTIC WOMEN.—CONTINUED.

"Mothers! in the name of religion and humanity, I charge you, teach your daughters *industry*. No matter how much of wealth, or beauty and refined accomplishments they have; without this virtue they are unfit to be either wives, or mothers, or members of society: without this their husbands, their children, the society of which they are to be members, will suffer a greater loss in respect to them than can be atoned for—greater than my pen shall attempt to describe.

"Never allow them to think that their hands are too good to perform any useful work, or that any task is too laborious for their perseverance to accomplish, or any study or art too hard for their minds and their industry to master. Let them early learn and ever remember the motto, 'Labor pertinax omnia vincit;' and let the great motives and encouragements to industry be kept constantly before them."—WINSLOW.

Some few years ago, gymnastics for boys, and calisthenics for girls, were loudly applauded for their beneficial results in physical education; but now, with other obsolete fashions, they seem to have passed away among the things that are forgotten, principally on account, no doubt, of the abuses to which, in the hands of ignorant instructers, they were liable. And it is, perhaps, well that it is so;

for both these sciences are taught us by Nature, and she is by far the safest guide. The most useful exercises of the body are those which strengthen the powers that will be needed in the business of life; and however necessary skill in the performance of difficult and unnatural bodily feats may be to those whose business it is to exhibit themselves for the amusement of the public, such as circus-riders, posture-masters, &c., it is worse than useless to our children, whom we are educating to become rational and useful men and women.

"Exercise of the body," says Combe, "is labour; and labour directed to a useful purpose is as beneficial to the corporeal organs, and far more pleasing to the mind than when undertaken for no end but the preservation of health." Nor is there any exercise or labour, we may add, better suited to woman, and more capable of rendering her healthy, happy, and useful, than that which is found in domestic employments. In these she is provided with labour which can be pursued without "too much muscular exertion," and in a field, too, where her mind as well as affections may be enlisted to relieve and cheer her in its performance. As we have before remarked, there is no sentiment which has been more productive of evil to the female character than the one, even more frequently acted upon than avowed, that idleness is the test of gentility. There is too much truth in the observation of a late writer, that indolence "may be regarded as one of the most besetting and dangerous vices of our young women of the present time. There is with multitudes of them an enormous waste of energy, physical, intellectual, and moral: the sin of burying the talent is with them a crying sin."

Look round upon the groups of young females who crowd our private parties or public balls; who lounge upon the sofa receiving visits, or throng the city promenades to exhibit their decorated persons or to make morning calls, and how many can you point out among them who have fulfilled one useful purpose of existence to themselves, to their families, or to society? And all this waste of time and of energy in the pursuit of folly is in the hope of becoming thereby candidates for matrimony, while by this very means they are unfitting themselves for the situation they are seeking to attain. Nor is this all: their efforts defeat the wished-for end, inasmuch as the habits of indolence and extravagance in which so many young women are brought up, deter a multitude of young men from becoming husbands, lest they should involve themselves in pecuniary embarrassment; and as wealthy young men are extremely rare, we see marriages in fashionable life every day becoming fewer; thus leaving in our cities a numerous class of finely-dressed, pretty, and accomplished young ladies, doomed to become disappointed "establishment-seekers," and to fade into fretful and repining " old maids." An intelligent, useful woman, who continues in a state of celibacy from choice or from disappointed affection, is an honoured and valuable member of society; but she whose youth has been spent in idleness and folly, and in seeking for a husband in crowded scenes of amusement, becomes a pitiable object—a burden to herself, and the jest and by-word of her acquaintance.

The cultivation of domestic habits is so important in every point of view, that it is a strange anomaly so few mothers should be found who fulfil their duty to their daughters in teaching them how to be happy and useful at home. Every wife knows, every mother painfully feels, her own need of sound health, persevering industry, and unfailing energy to carry her successfully through her various duties; and should not her most strenuous efforts be employed to secure these invaluable gifts to her offspring? Is she not aware, that to make her daughter beloved or useful in the conjugal or maternal relation, she must train her to be a " keeper at home," and to " guide the house," as the Scriptures direct? then why, oh! why does she permit her to spend her days in idleness, and her evenings among gay crowds of triflers?

Strange is it, that even fashionable mothers, those whose sole wish for their beautiful and accomplished daughters is that they should be admired, sought after, and won, should not understand that, to make any strong and permanent impressions, it is necessary that their darlings' persons should not be too frequently exhibited in public. Such is the love of novelty in human nature, that a face only occasionally seen among the unvarying, perpetual round of the same countenances nightly shining out at every assemblage, has an attraction more powerful than beauty, or wit, or accomplishments. " Match-making" mothers and " establishment-seeking" daughters cannot be ignorant that there is a charm even in the semblance of the retired virtues; and yet they cannot be contented at home, but must roam nightly from house to house, and frequent one crowd after another, in the vain hope of finding a matrimonial prize in that circling whirl where there are so few prizes, and so many, many blanks.

It is only by the cultivation of habits of industry and activity, and a careful preparation for domestic life, that the great result—a happy and well-ordered home—can be secured. And the importance of this has engaged the attention of the politician and moralist, as well as of the philanthropist. Not only does the moral power of such a home exhibit its effects upon the character of all its inmates, but it exercises an important and extensive influence upon society at large. "Women," says De Tocqueville, "are the protectors of morals. There is no country where the tie of marriage is so much respected as in America, or where conjugal happiness is more highly or worthily appreciated. In Europe, almost all the disturbances of society arise from their irregularities of domestic life. To despise the natural bonds and legitimate pleasures of home, is to contract a taste for excesses, a restlessness of heart, and the evil of fluctuating desires. Agitated by the tumultuous passions which frequently disturb his dwelling, the European is galled by the obedience which the legislative powers of the state exact. But when the American retires from the turmoil of public life to the bosom of his family, he finds in it the image of order and of peace. There his pleasures are simple and natural; his joys are innocent and calm; and as he finds that an orderly life is the surest path to happiness, he accustoms himself without difficulty to moderate his opinions as well as his tastes. While the European endeavours to forget his domestic troubles by agitating society, the American derives from his own home that love of order which he afterward carries with him into public affairs."

If it be true, then, that public benefit as well as private happiness are promoted by a home " of order and of peace," should not this fact arrest the attention of those women whose professed object is to reform the public morals by agitating society? Would not their patriotism be more effectively, as well as more appropriately exhibited, by endeavouring to pour oil upon the troubled waters, instead of adding to the tumult of their restless agitation? Let them learn from these sentiments of the reflecting De Tocqueville the *value of an American home*, and strive to exalt the nation by exhibiting under their own roof a model government: a government of order, where all the members occupy their appropriate stations, and fulfil the duties respectively belonging to them.

It is a question of great moment, Are such homes increasing among us, or are they gradually passing away? Do we find in a majority of our city homes, that their employments are natural and useful, their pleasures innocent and calm? "The tormenting passions" excited by the craving for wealth and display; "the restlessness of heart" that drives woman from her home to seek excitement in public places of resort; and "fluctuating desires," agitating her bosom, and leading her to sigh for the admiration of the gay world, or the notoriety of being an actor in public duties: have not these found their way into American as well as European homes? Human passions and desires are everywhere the same, though the objects to which they are directed may be different. If De Tocqueville attributes the agitations of European society to a disrelish for "the legitimate pleasures of home," and a consequent "restlessness of heart and taste for excesses," among European *men*, would he not have been less indiscriminate in his praises of American *women* had he discovered that there are those among them who are agitated by similar emotions?

When we see the restless feelings that disturb our fashionable homes, the heart-burnings and competitions among rival candidates for fashionable fame, the thirst for public display, the goading anxiety to keep up appearances without sufficient means, and the misery resulting from debts and insolvency; when we observe the frequent revolutions from poverty to affluence, and then from extravagance to ruin, that are continually taking place around us, and their calamitous effects upon families brought up in luxury and idleness, have we not reason to fear that our "homes of order and of peace" are rapidly disappearing? and may we not denounce, in terms of unmeasured reprobation, that tyranny of fashion which is making such fearful inroads upon our domestic peace and happiness? When we find, too, even religious women forsaking home duties for public avocations, and hear an American mother, with her infant in her arms, giving utterance to such complaints as these: "We cannot go to Congress; we cannot stand in the pulpit; *we cannot be known; we must toil at home;*" and when we know that this individual represents an increasing class, it is time for us to tremble for our homes. Powerful indeed must have been the effect of this perverted feeling, to lead a mother to the indulgence or expression of such a sentiment. Toil at home! yes, thanks to Him who made us, this is at once our duty and our privilege; and may He, of his goodness, make every woman feel that it is also her highest happiness and her truest dignity.

To those who observe the "signs of the times" in the present disturbed state of society throughout the civilized world, it is matter of interesting inquiry how far woman has contributed to it by mingling in its agitations. Has she acted right in this? or would it not have been the part of true wisdom in her to have kept aloof from these excitements? and by cultivating her mind, strengthening her judgment, and purifying her heart by intellectual and religious self-training, would she not have enabled herself to become a greater benefactor to her race than by joining in the strife? By calmly viewing these tumults from the retirement of her home, she could form a juster estimate of the true and the right than by entering the public arena and participating in the contest? Passions and prejudices are generated in the midst of all excitements, and the loftiest minds become clouded by their exhalations; so that we shall see a dispassionate hearer, even of moderate abilities, a better judge of truth in such cases than the most gifted orator. Woman, too, is exposed to much greater danger than man when she engages in the various exciting questions of the day, as she is generally less deliberate in judgment, and more liable to be led wrong, from her quick susceptibilities, her ardent feelings, and her ready credulity. The sanctuary of domestic life is to her the place of safety as well as the "post of honour." From this quiet and secure point of observation she can look abroad with intelligent interest and calm reflection on the conflicting elements around her, dispassionately weigh opposing opinions, and study how she may best fulfil her part in promoting the spiritual and intellectual advancement of society. She will then conclude, that, as the helpmate of man, she can best serve the great interests of humanity, not by rushing into the public arena to add feverishness to his excitements, but by shedding upon him, in his hours of home repose, the calm, clear light of truth, of peace, and of virtue. It should be her endeavour to prepare her husband and sons for true usefulness in life. Instead of urging them to the pursuit of wealth, to gratify a selfish desire for display, she should endeavour to moderate this passion, to which there are already too many incentives. Instead of exciting their ambition for place and power, already too active, she should seek to persuade them that true wisdom consists in being contented with the station which Providence has allotted to them.

Whenever her husband or her sons are in peril of being led from the paths of strict honesty by the force of worldly example or by the *current maxims of trade,* let her hold up to their view those uncompromising principles of integrity established by Him who has pronounced a curse upon every species of unfair dealing between man and man, and thus endeavour to strengthen their wavering resolutions, by exhibiting to them the speciousness and the danger of those precepts which have no foundation but in worldly expediency. Should she at any time find them entering upon the crooked paths of dissimulation or of political intrigue, or becoming the advocates of some popular error in the hope of obtaining popular favour, let her remind them that the enduring respect of the people can only be secured by undeviating consistency and single-hearted honesty. But if, in earnestly labouring to do good to their fellow-men, they should become discouraged by finding

F

their efforts unjustly requited, encountering only opposition and obloquy even from those whom they are seeking to benefit, then let her bid them never despair in a righteous cause, but press perseveringly onward, alike regardless of the fear or the favour of man, and firmly relying upon God for a blessing upon their endeavours. Let her point them to Him, who, though despised and rejected of men, desisted not from his labours of love, and whose benevolent precepts are recorded for the encouragement and direction of all who confess his name: "Bless them that curse you, do good to them that hate you, and pray for them which despitefully use you and persecute you."

To woman it belongs, also, to elevate the intellectual character of her household, to kindle the fires of mental activity in childhood, and to keep them steadily burning with advancing years. "It is in educating the women of your country," says Mademoiselle Montgolfier, in a letter to one of our female writers, "that its future is prepared. It is by this that the land will be purified, where the men are too much absorbed by material interests. The intellectual life of America seems to have passed into the souls of the women." This may appear somewhat extravagant; but whether the fact be so or not, there can be no doubt that "intellectual life" should have an existence in the souls of American women. The men of our country, as things are constituted among us, find but little time for the cultivation of science and general literature—studies so eminently calculated to refine the mind and purify the taste, and which furnish so exhaustless a fund of elevated enjoyment to the heart. And this is the case even with those who have acquired a fondness for intellectual pursuits in early life. The absorbing passion for gain, and the pressing demands of business, engross their whole attention. Thus the merchant becomes a merchant, and nothing more; and the mind of the lawyer is little else than a library of cases and precedents, of legal records and commentaries. The physician loses sight of the scientific studies to which his profession so naturally directs him, contents himself with the same beaten track, and becomes a mere practitioner or operator. And the mechanic and agriculturist too often settle down into mere manual labourers, by suffering practical details wholly to occupy their minds as well as their bodies. The only relief to this absorbing devotion to "material interests" is found in the excitement of party politics.

These two engross the whole moral, intellectual, and physical man; and, to be convinced of this, we need not follow the American to his place of business or to political meetings—we have only to listen to his fireside conversation. It might be supposed that the few waking hours he spends at home in the bosom of his family, he would delight to employ upon such subjects as would interest and improve his wife and children, and that he would avail himself of these opportunities to refresh his wearied mind with new matters of thought. But in place of this, what is the perpetual theme of his conversation? Business and politics, six per cent., bank discounts, stock-jobbing, insolvencies, assets, liabilities—cases at court, legal opinions and decisions—neuralgia, gastric irritation, fevers, &c.—Clay, Webster, the Bank bill, and other political topics of the day: these are the subjects incessantly talked about by the male members of the family when at home, and which the females, of course, are neither expected to take any special interest in nor to understand. Or perhaps the wife may take her turn in relating the history of the daily vexations she experiences in her household arrangements, while the husband's eye is gazing on vacancy, or his mind is occupied by his business cares. Woman should be made to take an intelligent interest in her husband's affairs, and may be benefited by a knowledge of the value of money, its best mode of investment; or by being instructed in the laws of physiology and of hygiene; but she can receive neither pleasure nor profit from hearing the cabalistic terms familiar only to the initiated in the mysteries of financiering, or the occult words and phrases which the professional man employs to communicate his knowledge or the results of his observations. The husband should doubtless sympathize with the wife in her domestic trials; but he cannot, nor ought he to, become interested in every trivial vexation she may meet with. There should, then, be some common ground on which both may meet with equal pleasure and advantage to themselves and to their offspring; and what is there so appropriate to this end as *intellectual pursuits*?

What a certain writer has said of sons, may also be said, with equal truth, of many husbands: "they seem to consider their homes as mere places of boarding and lodging;" and, we may add, forget that it is the dwelling-place of their wives and children. So long as they provide for the physical wants of their families, they think their duty is fulfilled; as though shelter, food, and clothing could satisfy the necessities of immortal minds. They are liberal, perhaps, even to profusion, in surrounding their families with all that can minister to physical comfort, and the indulgence of vanity and pride, but they neglect to excite or to satisfy the more exalted desire for intellectual adorning and spiritual improvement. It is here our men are wanting; and female influence must supply the defect. A mother should sedulously cultivate the intellectual tastes of her children, and surround them with objects calculated to stimulate and gratify their ambition for knowledge. Her own mind should not only be richly stored with the wisdom of the past, but she should keep herself familiar with the current literature of the day, with the progress of science, and the new and useful truths it is constantly bringing to light. Out of all this fulness of knowledge she should communicate freely to her children, and labour by her conversation gently to draw her husband away from his contracted sphere of thought, to enter with her upon a more extended field of observation and reflection. She should entice him to forget his business and his politics, and to devote the few hours he spends at home to those higher pleasures of the mind, which will not only yield a delightful refreshment at the time, but enable him to return with renewed vigour to the routine of his daily labours.

Nor should woman be indifferent to the affairs of her country. She should never appear, indeed, as a partisan politician or a political disputant; but she should study the theory of the government under which she lives, and learn to respect its authority and to venerate its free institutions. She should look, however, only upon those immutable *principles* of freedom and justice which aim at "the greatest good to the greatest number," and never suffer herself to become interested in the shifting policy, the cunning devices, and the temporary expedients to which political partisans resort to secure their own ascendency, often, it is to be feared, with little consideration for the lasting welfare of their country. She should study rather the science of politics, than those vexed questions which spring mostly from the delusions of self-interest—the true reading of the text-book, and not the glosses of prejudiced or biased interpreters.

Nor should she seek to acquire this knowledge in order to proclaim her opinions to the world, but that she may be the better qualified to train up her sons in the love of their country and of their fellow-men, by instilling into their minds the lofty and generous principles of liberty and of equal rights, and a profound regard for just laws and rightful authority. "It seems now to be conceded," says Mrs. Sigourney, "that the vital interests of our country may be aided by the zeal of mothers. A barrier to the torrent of corruption, and a guard over the strongholds of knowledge and of virtue, may be placed by the mother as she watches over her cradled son. Let her come forth with vigour and vigilance at the call of her country, not like Boadicea in her chariot, but like the mother of Washington, feeling that the first lesson of every incipient ruler should be 'how to obey.' The degree of her diligence in preparing her children to be good subjects of a just government, will be the true measure of her patriotism. While she labours to pour a pure and heavenly spirit into the hearts that open around her, she knows not but she may be appointed to rear some future statesman for her nation's helm, or priest for the temple of Jehovah."

While such high duties and prerogatives may be exercised by woman in being a "keeper at home," with what propriety can she consider the domestic circle as being too circumscribed for her energies? Were she never to cross its threshold, she would find ample scope for her highest powers of intellect and action, and momentous responsibilities more than sufficient to occupy all her time and attention. It is from the false and pernicious sentiment that it is a degradation "to toil at home," that so many women of the present day are fast losing their domestic character. Home duties and employments have, indeed, become so intimately associated in their minds with the more mechanical labours of the house, that many females attach no other idea to them. It is true that these come within the sphere of those duties; but then there are other, higher, and less material interests connected with them—those which concern the imperishable minds committed to their charge. And even the minor labours, so distasteful to the indolent, the fastidious, and the fashionable—the daily routine of sweeping, dusting, and cooking, of making and mending apparel, &c.—even these become divested of their apparent insignificance when viewed in their relation to the important considerations of health, comfort, and order. True as it may be in England, to quote the remark of a late English writer, "that money can purchase the aid of a sempstress and a cook, but cannot buy maternal respect and influence;" yet in this country, at least, experienced housekeepers find that even the highest wages rarely can obtain such help in the different departments of household economy, as will dispense with the vigilant superintendence of the mistress of the family. However unladylike or vulgar these occupations may appear to the pseudo-refined, there are, in fact, but few professions or employments, even among men, which do not include many details that are disagreeable in themselves, but which, nevertheless, are far from being looked upon as contemptible, inasmuch as they are the necessary means to important results, and cannot be dispensed with. What, for example, should we think of a physician, were he to shrink with affected nicety from the investigation of the pathology of disease, because the methods by which it must be conducted are, perhaps, not of the most agreeable nature; or should he count it beneath his dignity to prepare the medicines he administers? And, again, are any of the duties which females are called upon to perform more apparently menial than that required of a surgeon in the navy, to inspect the copper utensils after they have been cleaned, to see if they are in a fit condition for the preparation of food? But he does not despise this part of his office as degrading, for he knows that the life and health of the whole crew depend upon its faithful performance. If right-minded men thus dignify the littleness of detail, should not woman do the same? Surely the health and the physical comfort of her husband and children should be considered of sufficient importance by every female to induce her to attend to the cleanliness and ventilation of her apartments, and to the rules of dietetics necessary to be observed in preparing proper food in a proper manner, so as to furnish the most healthful nutriment. To see that these things are rightly done is the duty of woman; and in their proper performance there is dignity, and not degradation. One great reason why the minor duties of women are looked upon as mean and servile, is that they have been given up to servants, and are considered as exclusively belonging to them. But men who have correct notions of their responsibilities do not thus delegate their lesser duties to hirelings, regarding them as involving considerations far too important to admit of their being intrusted to ignorance and incapacity; and where woman correctly appreciates the importance of hers, she will not so readily relinquish them to others.

In thus exposing the folly and shortsightedness of treating any duty as contemptible, and in enforcing the necessity of a vigilant attention to whatever is embraced within the range of duty, it is by no means intended to be implied that the mistress of a family can be its sole manual labourer. That a woman can properly perform the offices of sempstress, housemaid, cook, and nurse in her family, so as to leave time for her higher conjugal and maternal duties, will, to say the least, admit of doubt. Indeed, wholly to dispense with the assistance of domestic servants in the present condition of society would seem to be impracticable. That most of the difficulties and trials of housekeeping arise from the ignorance and faithlessness of servants, is evident from the almost universal complaints we hear on every side; and yet, though all acknowledge these evils, they are considered for the most part as necessary ones, and few are found willing to admit the possibility of getting along without them. With the exception of the wives and daughters of our labouring population, who have been trained to activity and industry, and have thus acquired sound health and untiring physical energies, most of our females are slavishly dependant upon their domestics; and that this dependance is seen and felt by the latter, is abundantly evident from their increasing exactions, and their often repeated threats of leaving their place: threats which upon the slightest pretence they do not hesitate to execute. Every housekeeper knows that a competent domestic in any department feels her own consequence, and that in most cases there is but a feeble hold on her services, except where there exists an attachment produced by long residence. Hence we find many a mistress of a family who is almost afraid to reprove even where reproof is necessary, or to correct a growing abuse lest she should lose a servant whose aid is valuable to her; and she cannot but feel degraded in her own estimation by being obliged, as it were, to submit to such a state of things. A reformation is certainly needed here, but where shall the reform begin? Shall we tamely submit to this slavish dependance upon domestic servants, or shall we endeavour so to improve their character and qualifications as to lessen the evil? or shall we endeavour so to educate the rising generation as to enable them to dispense with the troublesome aid now required, by bringing up our daughters to active industry, and thus securing to them the physical strength and health necessary to this independence.

In speaking of domestic servants, Mr. Sedgwick says: "This is a class that exists in every civilized community in the world, and always will exist." Under existing circumstances, indeed, division of labour would seem to be scarcely less necessary in household affairs, than in the various departments of trade and manufactures. And if, as the above-mentioned writer again remarks, "common sense teaches that the time of a President of the United States ought not to be spent in boiling his own teakettle, and that a man whose business it is to administer justice as a judge, or set broken bones as a surgeon, has not the time to cleanse his own horse and stables," does it not also lead us to the conclusion, that a mother with a young infant claiming her care, can hardly be expected to be able faithfully to discharge her duty to it, attend to the physical, moral, and intellectual training of her older children, and at the same time perform all the manual labours of her household? This would seem to be impossible, under the most favourable circumstances as to health, active and industrious habits, and the best management. Either her higher or her minor duties must be neglected or imperfectly performed. The wives of the labouring classes, who do all their own work, and do it faithfully, have their domestic arrangements confined within a smaller circle. They seldom exercise that watchful care over their children which others deem necessary, but send them to school to keep them out of the way, or suffer them to run hither and thither with such associates as they may happen to meet, and to be exposed to dangers on which they have but little leisure to reflect. The highest duties of the mother, therefore, and " the maid of all work" would appear to be incompatible. Not that any woman, even of the most refined education, or possessing the most gifted genius, is degraded by doing her own washing, cooking, housecleaning, &c.; but it seems not to be possible that she should perform them all with her own hands, and have time for the more important duties resting on her as a wife and a mother. Still, admitting this, it is not the less incumbent on her to superintend and direct all these matters.

A great change must be made in our houses, our education, and our entire style of living, before we can hope to do without this assistance. There is an immense waste of time and labour in useless and extravagant cookery, in preparing superfluous articles of dress, in taking care of unnecessary furniture, in making clean and keeping clean large and inconveniently constructed houses, and a greater number of apartments than is needful. With more judicious arrangements, much of the work now required to be performed in our households might be dispensed with, without any diminution of comfort, neatness, or order. The labours to accomplish what is really necessary bear but a small proportion to those exacted by self-indulgence and ostentation; and that woman who shall strive to dispense with the non-essentials in her domestic economy, and expose the folly of paying for useless labour, will prove herself the best of *female reformers*, and be entitled to the gratitude of her sex. What should we think of a system of household management that required one servant to be continually passing up and down stairs, and another perpetually engaged in pouring water from one vessel into another, while the attention of the mistress of the family was constantly required to see that these things were properly done? And yet how much time and labour are often wasted in an equally unprofitable manner, to as little good purpose, and with as little real benefit to the members of the household. Nay, even in the work that is absolutely necessary, how many precious hours are thrown away in our circuitous modes of performing a task that, with greater practical ingenuity, might be shortened to a few minutes. If a small portion only of the inventive mechanical genius which has been employed for the saving of labour in our manufactories, had been directed to the abridgment of female labour in our houses, the improvement of our sex would have advanced with greater rapidity; for it is with industrious housekeepers as with the labouring class in the community: while so much of their time and energies are necessarily occupied in providing for the wants of the body, their intellectual, moral, and spiritual interests must be neglected. When household work is abridged, and made lighter by better mechanical contrivances; when women shall be trained, both physically and intellectually, for a more efficient and more enlightened fulfilment of all their duties; and when both men and women shall consent to live in a style more conformable to the simplicity of republican institutions, then, and not till then, will there be a possibility of dispensing with domestic servants.

Dr. Alcott, we believe, is the only writer who

has advocated the entire relinquishment of hired assistance in household economy; and however unfavourably some of his theories may have been received, yet he is entitled to our gratitude for his efforts in woman's behalf. If he has urged upon her the importance of attending to minor duties, he has sought also to accomplish her for the fulfilment of those of a higher order. If he would have the mistresses of families take upon themselves more of household manual labour than they have hitherto been accustomed to, he has at the same time pointed out the means of greatly abridging these labours, by returning to a more simple mode of living. And here, without advocating the abstemiousness of Grahamism, every reflecting woman must admit that the time and money consumed in preparing luxurious articles of food, merely for the gratification of the palate, to the serious injury of health, is a great evil, and one which loudly calls for correction. Whatever difference of opinion there may be on the subject of dietetics in other respects, in this all judicious persons must agree, that good plain cookery of simple food is not only a great economy of time and money, but far more conducive to health than luxurious viands, or the multifarious mixtures called *French dishes*.

There is nothing of which we hear old housekeepers more frequently complain, than of the great change which has taken place in the character of domestic servants within the last twenty or thirty years; and this is doubtless true. They are no longer as submissive to the will of their employers as they formerly were. But if they assume so much independence, and are so prompt to assert their rights, inconvenient as it may be in many respects to the comforts of housekeepers, we must recollect that this class is only undergoing a change in common with every other. They participate in the general movement that is making in regard to " human rights ;" and as the just limits of authority and obedience, and the true relations of the different orders in society seem not to be fully settled, we need not be surprised that they should, in many instances, expect and demand what their employers may deem unwarrantable privileges. There is a clashing of views between the assumed rights of two different classes. On the one side we see the ancient opinions and prejudices derived from the feudal law of baron and vassal still maintaining their ground; and, on the other, the masses of the community striving to burst the barriers of *caste*, and to resist every exaction of arbitrary power. It is a contest between the two great principles of *law* and *liberty*, both equally important in the proper regulation of every community, households as well as nations, and the respective limits of which are yet to be definitively adjusted.

One great change to be observed in the character of domestic service in this country is, that the contract between mistress and servant is now one for *labour* rather than for *time*. Formerly servants were supposed to surrender their whole time during the period of their service, and considered it all at the disposal of their employers; and when they asked for leisure it was as a favour, and not as a right. But at present it seems to be understood that particular services, or only a certain amount of work, is to be required, and that, when this is performed, they are entirely at liberty to dispose of the remainder of their time according to their own pleasure. Such, at least, is the case in all our large cities, as is experienced by most housekeepers; and many of the best servants are no less tenacious in maintaining their rights in this respect, than faithful in discharging what they consider to be their duty to their employers. Housekeepers, by refusing to admit this as a right, often thus deprive themselves of valuable domestics, and are kept in a state of constant irritation by these opposing claims.

Besides this, domestic servants at the present day prefer stipulating for the performance of certain specified duties, and are generally found unwilling to do anything that does not strictly belong to their department. Another claim, also, is beginning to be advanced, the right to receive visiters; and this is frequently brought forward and insisted upon as a preliminary condition before they will consent to enter into service. Few housekeepers are prepared to concede all these demands as rights, and hence the continual disagreement between mistresses and servants. The latter are well aware that their assistance cannot be dispensed with, and thus, feeling their power, they seek to dictate their own terms. Instead, then, of vainly wishing to throw them back to their former state of submission, let us calmly examine what are the rights fairly belonging to them in the present state of society, and, after determining this, promptly admit them; while, in the mean time, we endeavour to convince them of their error where they are manifestly wrong, and where unreasonable and extravagant pretensions operate to the disadvantage of both parties. If this course be not adopted, the time is not far distant when it will be found expedient to dispense in a great measure with domestic help; and this will continue until both sides become better enlightened as to their true relative position and their best interests. This experiment is indeed already being made. There are many women of refined tastes and accomplished education, who, in different parts of our country, have chosen to become their own cooks and housemaids rather than be surrounded with incompetent or troublesome assistants.

Dr. Alcott considers the system of keeping servants in our families as highly anti-republican, and asks, " Do not all conscientious parents know that, by having a class of persons about them whom they are accustomed to regard as inferiors, they are fostering in their own bosoms, as well as cherishing in the bosoms of their children, a feeling which is as contrary to true republicanism as light is to darkness?" Few probably will be found either sufficiently patriotic or self-denying to assent to his views in this particular; but all must admit the validity of the following objections urged by him against the custom, viz., "that servants are bad teachers and educators," and, as such, injurious to our own character and that of our children; that "they are costly," and, consequently, that a sound economy would lead us to do without them. As to the expensiveness of domestic servants, all housekeepers, even the least reflecting, will fully agree that their high wages, the division of labour among them rendering it necessary to keep more help than is absolutely requisite, and their extravagance, waste, and carelessness, which nothing but the most unremitting vigilance can lessen or prevent, are reasons sufficiently powerful to make all heads of families feel the force of this objection. He also regards the practice as anti-Christian, from its unfavourable effect upon the temper and disposition of the heads of families as well as their domestics, and adds, "It is a state of temptation into which a Christian should not wish to be led." That the "chronic evil of corrupt domestic servitude," as a writer in the London Quarterly terms it, is one of the most prolific sources of irritation, and of departure from the meek and quiet spirit enjoined in the Gospel, is a truth which every Christian manager of a household must painfully feel; yet may not the fault lie in the circumstances attending the relation rather than in the relation itself? And might not a remedy be found in a mutual reformation, and in a better education of both parties for the proper discharge of their respective duties to each other?

Notwithstanding the general complaint of the trouble experienced from servants, it is evident that the number employed is continually becoming larger. Not only do we find more domestics in fashionable families than were formerly thought necessary, but the practice of hiring help has become common among those who, a few years ago, found sufficient time and ability to do their own work. Dr. Alcott on this subject remarks, "That many families in the country towns of Massachusetts employ from one to three hired servants, who but a few years ago, had they employed but a single one, would probably have been ridiculed." The same thing may be observed in most of our Atlantic cities and villages, where we find the wives of journeymen mechanics and labourers following in this respect the pernicious example set by the wealthy, or those who are making a show of being such.

Whether the practice of employing more domestics than are actually needed be, as Dr. Alcott observes, "an imitation of foreign manners and customs," or whether it arises from neglected physical education, and a want of training to domestic employments among our females of all classes, we know not, though it may be in part ascribed perhaps to both these causes. The result is an unfavourable indication of our social condition, and one among many evidences of the extravagance and ostentation everywhere prevailing. As statistics have been given, showing a most shameful waste of money in the vast sums expended by us for imported finery in silks, jewelry, embroidery, &c., it is to be regretted that so good an opportunity of ascertaining the number of domestic servants we employ should have been lost, by omitting this item in the census just taken. In the United Kingdom of Great Britain and Ireland, by the census of 1831, the number of domestic servants was considerably over a million.

The female servants were:

  In England . . . 77 in a thousand.
  In Wales . . . . 102 " "
  In Scotland . . . 88 " "
  In Ireland . . . 63 " " .
Total number of female servants, 923,646.

The male servants were:

In England . . . 16 in a thousand of the male population.
In Wales . . . . 8½ " " " "
In Scotland . . . 17½ " " " "
In Ireland . . . . 26 " " " "
 Whole number of male servants, 211,966.

Had the number of domestic servants with us been ascertained, it is probable the proportion would have been still greater; for, although few families have sufficient wealth to maintain a train of servants as numerous as those employed in single families in Great Britain, yet, from the more general distribution of wealth in the United States, the number of families keeping domestic assistants must, we think, be larger than in the United Kingdom. And the many unnecessary servants employed in our houses, their high wages and wasteful habits, if the results could be accurately estimated, would be found to form a large item in the list of extravagances for which the females of our country are responsible.

Housekeepers bitterly feel the evils connected with the present system of domestic service, and yet supinely submit to them, in the belief that they are unavoidable, without reflecting how far they might be removed by a judicious reformation. Thus, if we cannot altogether dispense with them, we may materially lessen their number; while, by efforts to educate them in a knowledge of their duties, by respecting their just rights, and by treating them with the kindness they ought to receive from us, we might greatly elevate them as a class. If, as an

English writer observes, "we depend upon them for the cleanliness and security of home, with the comfort of every hour spent in it; for the care of children, the preservation of property, and the maintenance of the respectability of the house," then surely self-interest, if no higher motive can animate us, should render us assiduous and persevering in our efforts for their improvement. And yet *they are a sadly neglected class.* Being inmates of our families, and having constant intercourse with them, they may justly claim our most earnest attention to their intellectual and moral advancement; and still, are there not Christian females among us, who, while they take a deep interest in the efforts that are being made to send the Gospel to the heathen, are almost wholly inattentive to the spiritual wants and deficiencies of those who are in daily attendance on them?

Is it not strange, that among all the societies of the day, not one should have been formed for the intellectual and moral improvement of domestic servants, and for instructing them in household employments? What a blessing would it bring upon our homes, if, in addition to proper religious and mental training, girls looking forward to domestic service could be enlightened in regard to the duties and responsibilities belonging to such a situation? But still, though much good may be done by acting upon masses either of adults or children, yet the most efficient and certain influence for good can only be exercised by one individual upon another, as, for example, in the relation of mistress and servant. And until housekeepers learn to look upon their domestics in a higher light than as mere machines intended to go through a certain round of labour, with but little regard either to their feelings or welfare, the present evils will continue to be experienced. When the managers of families shall better appreciate and more scrupulously discharge their duty in these particulars, then, and not till then, can they expect to find domestics as faithful, attached, and efficient as they are anxious to have them.

But, in addition to the evils just spoken of, there is often the still more lamentable one of ignorance and inefficiency in the housekeeper herself. A mistress skilled in the knowledge and practice of housewifery may do much even with indifferent servants, or may be able to select good ones; for, after all, they are more frequently to be met with than the complaints so generally made would lead us to suppose. But a woman who has been brought up in idleness and self-indulgence cannot cast off her responsibilities as easily as she can dismiss an unsatisfactory domestic; and she must ever be subject to great disadvantages on account of her own incompetency, as even the best servants will lose much of their value when placed under her control and direction. Strange is it that domestic economy, upon the proper understanding and practice of which so much of our happiness depends, should be so little studied. There is no want of writers or instructers where other subjects are to be considered, but how few have given any attention to this? With the exception of Dr. Alcott's writings, the work of Mrs. Parks, and a few pages here and there in some other authors, the only books we have in relation to this subject are family receipt-books, as though the art of cookery and the preparation of expensive dishes were the most important part of household management. But domestic economy, in its true sense, embraces everything pertaining to woman's duties in domestic life. It relates not only to her duties as a housekeeper, but also as a wife and mother; and by studying it aright she will be enabled to discharge all her responsibilities arising out of these relations, without permitting one thing to infringe upon another, and in a manner that each duty shall have its due share of attention, in proportion to its true relative importance; for no one of her numerous duties can be neglected or carelessly performed without serious injury to the well-being of her family.

Good housewifery is, indeed, an important branch of this science, and Mrs. Willard has given us the following definition of it: "Housewifery teaches properly to superintend or perform all those operations which are necessary to the well-ordering of the internal concerns of a family. It teaches the best method of preserving and preparing food, as regards economy, health, and gratification of the appetite. It requires the keeping in a state of neatness and order the rooms, furniture, and clothes for the use of the family; and also the governing and managing a household, so that the subordinate agents shall know their proper place and business, that thus everything may be done in season without bustle or confusion."

There are many good housekeepers who have made themselves perfect by long practice, and yet how few are capable of imparting such knowledge to the ignorant and inexperienced, as will save them from the numerous mistakes and difficulties which they themselves have had to encounter? It is something more than mere housekeepers that we want here; we need teachers—intelligent, judicious, experienced teachers; women capable of viewing the whole ground of domestic duty; who feel alive to all the responsibilities of their sex as wives and mothers, and yet are not insensible to the importance and dignity of the housekeeping department. Such women there are; and let them come forward and discharge their duty to the rising female generation, by showing them how women can be good housekeepers without disregarding any of their higher obligations, either to their husbands, or children, to society, or to themselves.

We should be grateful for instruction, from whatever source it may come; but it is the reflecting, experienced, sympathizing woman who is fitted to be the most efficient teacher of her sex. Let all such, then, feel it to be their duty to labour in the great cause of female improvement, and to follow the apostle's injunction in being "teachers of good things; that they may teach the young women to be discreet, chaste, keepers at home, good, obedient to their own husbands; to be sober, to love their husbands, to love their children." Let them do what they can towards reforming the present generation. But if it shall be found a hopeless task to regenerate those who have been brought up in indolence and self-indulgence; who are fettered to their present style of living, and bound by innumerable chains to the tyranny of transatlantic customs, then let them do what they can to secure better things for the generation to come. Let them urge mothers to train up their daughters in habits of activity and of useful industry; to lift them above the folly of extravagance and of vain display, by cultivating in their minds a pure taste, and the love for republican simplicity; and while their daughters are made to aspire after the highest refinement and the most advanced intellectual attainments, let this truth be deeply impressed on their minds, that "a Christian is the highest style" of woman as well as "of man." Then, if these lessons be faithfully inculcated and practised, the daughters of America will be what woman in America ought to be: a model to her sex in every clime, exhibiting the effects of her country's *Liberty* in her freedom from the slavery of fashion, and of all the follies that once held her in bondage; and of her country's *Law*, in the beautiful harmony with which she moves in her appointed sphere, shedding the bright radiance of moral and intellectual light upon a home of order and of peace.

CHAPTER III.

FASHIONABLE WOMEN.

"Here we cannot but feel the necessity of subjecting our gallantry to our reason, and inquiring how far the indifference to what is great, and the passion for what is frivolous, may be occasioned by the present tone of that influence which women naturally exercise in this country, as in all modern civilized communities. Whoever is disposed to give accurate attention to the constitution of fashion (which fashion in the higher classes is, in other words, the spirit of society), must at once perceive how largely fashion is formed, and how absolutely it is governed by the gentler sex. Our fashion may, indeed, be considered the aggregate of the opinions of woman. In order to account for the tone that fashion receives, we have but to inquire into the education bestowed upon woman.

"We hold that feminine influence, however secret, is unavoidably great. * * * Even in limited circles, how vast that influence in forming the national character, which some deny because it is secret! how evident a proof of the influence of those whose minds you will not enlarge, in that living which exceeds means; so wretched in its consequences, so paltry in its object! Who shall say that the whole comfortless, senseless, heartless system of ostentation has no cause—not in woman, if you like, but in the education we give her?"—*Edinburgh Review*.

By fashionable women we mean those females who live especially for the "world;" who sacrifice home comforts and home duties for the sake of ostentatious display, and who find more pleasure in the attractions of society than in their own families. The characteristics of this class are love of dress, fondness for visiting, a passion for fine houses and fine furniture, and for all the frivolities pertaining to an extravagant style of living. The appellation "fashionable people" is usually applied to those who are considered as belonging to the *élite*, or select few—to the first circles in fashionable life; and who are the *leaders of the Ton*. But our definition has a more extended meaning, and will embrace *followers* as well as leaders; in short, all those who exhibit the like characteristic traits, whether they be the gaudily-dressed daughters of the mechanic, or the more richly-attired wife and daughters of the professional man, the banker, or the merchant.

Though the domestic class in our country can happily still claim the largest number, if we embrace the whole of its widely-extended population, yet the fashionable class is rapidly increasing, and has a much greater and more perceptible influence upon society at large. It is an influence, too, no less extensive than powerful; and to be convinced of this, we need only observe "the spirit of society" as exhibited in our cities, towns, and villages, and even in the green retreats of our rural abodes:

> "The town has tinged the country; and the stain
> Appears a spot upon a vestal's robe,
> The worse for what it soils. The fashion runs
> Down into scenes still rural; but, alas!
> Scenes rarely graced with rural manners now."

Were its only effects the silly fondness for shining gewgaws and gilded bawbles—a taste, by-the-way, most strikingly displayed in the child and the savage—we might perhaps smile at these silly fancies, so indicative of the want of intellectual elevation. But the evil assumes a startling magnitude when we reflect that it is so often *wives* and *mothers*—beings possessing fearful responsibilities—who devote themselves to these follies; who thus pervert woman's influence—that mighty instrument given to be employed for the moral advancement of the race—by abusing it to the degradation of both sexes, by exciting in them an "indifference to what is great, and a passion for what is frivolous." It is not only the perfumed foplings found in our drawing-room coteries who thus become enslaved to the dominion of fashion, but our men of business and of talent are insensibly drawn into its service. A fine house and splendid equipage have become no less attractive to man than to woman, and their glitter is equally fascinating in his eyes. We find him discoursing as eloquently upon carpets and curtains, dinner-services and plate, as could the veriest female slave to fashion, and as willingly circumscribing his library or his cabinet to add to the dimensions and gorgeousness of his drawing-room.

It is not individual character alone that is degraded by this " passion for the frivolous ;" it enters into our national character more deeply than the superficial observer has ever imagined. Whence arises the feverish thirst for wealth, with the eager and too often dishonourable struggles to obtain it, so universally recognised as one of our most striking national traits? It is not avarice that causes our men to sacrifice health, mental cultivation, and sometimes honour and integrity, and even life itself, in its pursuit. No; their lavish expenditures abundantly show that it is not the miser's passion for hoarding which stimulates their efforts. What is the object, then, to which this wealth, so earnestly sought for, is to be applied? To the gratification of a craving appetite for display; to be squandered in ostentatious living: and to be convinced of this, we have but to observe to what purposes the first funds that can be spared from business or from professional incomes are usually applied. They are invested in the fine house with its fashionable furniture; and to this must shortly be added the dashing equipage and the expensive entertainment. How much wiser would it be to employ such surplus means in providing for the better education of children; in supplying them with those aids to their advancement which would improve their intellect and refine their taste: the extensive library; the well-stored cabinet; the chymical and philosophical apparatus; chef-d'œuvres in painting and sculpture, or the choicest specimens from the burin of the engraver. But, instead of this, we see far greater sums than would be required for these objects worse than wasted in tinsel ornaments to attract the eyes of "stupid starers" in the fashionable world, and the real comfort, true happiness, and highest interests of their families sacrificed to a "senseless, heartless system of extravagant and ostentatious living, wretched in its consequences, and paltry in its object."

To which of the sexes are we to look as the primary agent in upholding this widespread evil; in planting in our soil this poisonous exotic, which withers every fresh and living principle of moral and intellectual life that comes within its blighting influence? It is, we fear, to woman! It is to gratify her craving for display that man labours to procure these shining bawbles, that he may lay them at her feet. In a community of male members alone (if such were to be found), there would probably be *too little* regard for outward show; for wherever men are isolated from female society, they are apt to neglect even their personal appearance. And among the pioneers of our Western wilds, we discover that it is woman who most bitterly feels the privation of former luxuries, and who is least easily reconciled to the rude cabin, with its pine tables and uncarpeted floors, though it may, after all, contain whatever is necessary to satisfy a rational love of order and neatness, and a correct taste. If it be woman, then, who is chiefly chargeable with the introduction and support of these errors, it is to her we must look for their correction. She must be made to feel the sin and the folly of that fashionable extravagance she has unhappily been so instrumental in encouraging; which has spread itself like a flood over our fair land, and desolated so many of our American homes.

When we consider the ruin of private fortunes and character, and the public embarrassments that have been brought upon us by reckless speculation, destroying the happiness of families, and threatening the overthrow of our national peace and prosperity, have we not reason to denounce the vehement passion for gain out of which these evils have arisen, and which is chiefly fostered and upheld by our ostentatious and unnatural modes of living? These are the vampyres that are draining the very life-blood of our republican integrity and simplicity, and with the tyranny of Mezentius have bound the repulsive carcass of fashionable society in an unnatural union to our living, healthy, and vigorous government. What an anomaly, in a country whose political institutions are all based upon economy, simplicity, and equal rights, to see an insatiable desire for wealth and costly display!

Politicians are heard crying aloud for economy in the management of the public interests, while they present in their own households an example of extravagance. But true patriotism should have but one rule of action, bearing equally upon private and public affairs. It is matter of deep regret that so few of our eminent men have risen superior to the passion for ostentatious display. So thoroughly imbued, indeed, are all classes with this frivolous fondness for glitter and show, that we rarely find an individual who does not rest his claim to social distinction quite as much, nay, more, upon his style of living, his fashionable house, furniture, and equipage, than upon his talents, refinement, or education. And how seldom is it that we find in our social circles one who may be considered as truly personifying the majestic simplicity of our government. While our public men can so eloquently declaim about the moral sublimity of our plain republican institutions, and their superiority over the vain pomp and show of royalty, how many of them do we see bowing their necks under the yoke of European habits, fashion, and corruption, the necessary and inseparable appendages of those very governments they so loudly condemn.

It has been said that "the physical derangements of society are but the image and impress of its spiritual; while the heart continues sound, all other sickness is but superficial and temporary. False action is the fruit of false speculation: let the spirit of society be free and strong—that is to say, let true principles inspire the members of society—and then disorders cannot accumulate in its practice; each disorder will be promptly, faithfully inquired into, and remedied as it rises." This is our hope: that the heart of American society is still sound at the core; its spirit still strong and free, in despite of these outward appearances of transatlantic infection; and we trust that these incipient disorders will be faithfully inquired into and promptly remedied ere they shall have reached the vitals of the Republic.

When we lift the curtain which conceals the drama of private life, what scenes of wretchedness, folly, and crime are presented to us, occasioned by wasteful expenditure and an insane passion for fashionable show. Witness the innumerable instances of families by these causes plunged from affluence into the depths of poverty, whose situation is made tenfold more intolerable by the feelings of mortified pride, while their necessities inflict a deeper anguish from long-indulged habits of luxury and indolence. And on looking around upon the gorgeous and expensive embellishments with which the aspirants to fashionable distinction delight to decorate their dwellings, one might predict their downfall almost with the certainty of prophetic prescience. It is said that a father, while sadly gazing around on the splendours of the mansion of his son, whose fortune had risen from nothing with the suddenness of Aladdin's palace, sighed deeply and said, "I see written here, as plainly as Belshazzar saw the handwriting on the wall, 'To be sold by the sheriff.'" Inscribed on how many mansions in our land might we, with prophetic ken, read the same record, often to be fulfilled as suddenly as was the mystic writing that foretold the destruction of the proud King of the Chaldeans. Whenever we see the sudden accumulation of wealth speedily followed by a wasteful and extravagant style of living, we may regard it as almost a sure presage of bankruptcy and ruin. And yet, such is the utter recklessness produced by this passion for fashionable display, that men will not learn wisdom from the disastrous experience of others, but madly rush forward in their career of folly, in the vain hope that their fate will prove an exception to the general rule.

Were those who thus sin against reason and experience the only sufferers, there would, perhaps, be little to excite our sympathy; but here the innocent suffer more than the guilty. Extravagance is akin to dishonesty; for its effects are to rob the confiding creditor of his dues; and this frequently falls upon those least able to bear it. Indeed, such is the corrupting influence of this passion for costly show, that but few who yield to it retain their integrity unimpaired. And how many do we see, who, to keep up an appearance of splendour, resort to every species of wrong—from unpaid debt to knavish trickery, and sometimes forgery itself. This latter crime, once punishable with a felon's death, has of late years been by no means uncommon in fashionable life.

The passion for extravagance is remarked by foreigners to be no less characteristic of our countrymen than the passion for gain; and there is, doubtless, too much truth in the charge. It has been stated that the largest and most expensive mirrors made in France are for the American market; and this fact would seem to corroborate the observation of an eminent phrenologist, that *vanity* is as largely developed in the national character of America as is *pride* in that of England. American females in Europe are said to be noted for their extravagance, and for making expensiveness instead of taste their standard of fashionable perfection. The kind of extravagance, too, in which our fashionable women indulge, is of all others the most wasteful. The coroneted females of Europe expend immense sums for diamonds and other jewels; but these have an intrinsic value, and can at any time be converted into money; whereas our wealth is lavished upon fripperies that "perish in the using." They are of no value except so long as they are fashionable, which is never but for a very brief period; and when the capricious goddess that presides over these matters decrees some new mode, they are instantly thrown aside, to take their place, perhaps, on the shelves of the pawnbroker, or to decorate some old clothes shop.

The evidences of female extravagance in dress are not only seen in our city promenades and drawing-rooms, but are to be found in the records of our national and state governments. The enormous sums annually paid for French silks have been urged upon the floor of Congress as calling loudly for an increase of duties; and a governor of one of our states presents in his message the startling fact, that the money paid for this article alone in a single year is more "than it cost to build the Erie Canal." In the report of the Secretary of the Treasury for 1839, we find among the importations of that year the following items:

Thread and cotton lace	$1,213,672
Lace veils, shawls, and shades	345,490
Manufactures of silk and worsted	2,319,884
Silks	20,474,454!!!

Of all these articles, the amount exported to other markets was only $704,159, leaving the immense total of $23,649,341 for the consumption of the United States. Looking in the same report at the list of imported articles pertaining to science, taste, and literature, the following remarkable contrast is exhibited:

Philosophical apparatus	$10,168
Statuary, busts, and casts	2,330
Paintings, drawings, and etchings	4,542
Cabinets of coins and gems	none
Cabinets of medals and antiquities	none
Specimens in Botany	5,087

And the entire aggregate of books, maps, and charts amounts only to a little more than three hundred thousand dollars. Thus the amount of imports connected with the pursuits of science, literature, and the fine arts, was only 352,446 dollars, or but little more than one seventieth part the amount expended for gaudy articles of dress.

The writer of an article in the Democratic Review for 1839, on Philadelphia Banking, states that in a single year importations were made to the amount of nearly eleven millions of dollars in articles of which almost the whole value consisted in ornamental needlework, such as wrought muslins, embroidered handkerchiefs, and expensive laces.

These facts, recorded in state papers, and commented upon in our legislative halls and public journals, are to be received as so many cutting sarcasms upon the extravagance of American females. In these comments, from feelings of gallantry, no doubt, censure has been withheld from those to whom it is chiefly due. Let our women, then, magnanimously come forward, and with one accord frankly confess that the fault is theirs, resolving to use their utmost efforts to make amends for past folly by adopting a chaste simplicity of dress—one more in accordance with correct taste as well as economy, and thus redeem our national character from the stigma now resting upon it.

One of our own writers has asserted that, "Let the misery be what it may in the United States, there must be finery." It is this love of finery which is the prolific source of every kind of extravagance; while of all extravagance, that of dress is the silliest and most frivolous, and, except that of the table, the most wasteful. The wine-bibber, who melts his wealth in the cup, and quaffs it as recklessly as did Cleopatra the liquefied pearl; and the glutton or epicure, who, in imitation of the debased emperors of degenerate Rome, expends his fortune in rare and expensive dishes, both gain what they seek—a sensual gratification suited to their sensual natures; but the female who decks her person in superfluous finery defeats the very object she is supposed to be aiming at—the admiration of the other sex. We are ready to admit the powerful effect of dress in giving greater attractiveness to woman; still it is not the less certain that those females widely err who make extravagant finery the criterion of what dress should be. Excessive ornament lessens the effect of female beauty, while it renders a homely woman still more homely. In every circle she will invariably be most admired who is the most plainly attired. Two of our eminent artists enjoined the utmost simplicity of dress upon their daughters, as being more consonant to the principles of true taste, and more agreeable to the eye, on account of its harmony with the beautiful. And we have abundant evidence that in this respect natural taste is no less true in its instincts than where it has been ripened by cultivation; for simplicity in female costume meets with universal admiration. The only reason we can assign for the perverted taste exhibited by females in their passion for finery, and their inferiority to the other sex in this particular, is, that in the former this passion is fostered in infancy by every possible means, from the tawdry-dressed doll, to the ribands, necklaces, and furbelows with which their little persons are loaded; while in respect to the latter, cleanliness and neatness are considered the only requisites.

"Of all ways of spending money," says Sedgwick, in his Public and Private Economy, "few can be thought more contemptible than to load the head, neck, ears, body, fingers, and feet with a mass of finery and trumpery, created by immense labour, and to be discarded forever on the first turn in the fashions; if done by the rich, it is extreme folly; if by the poor, certain ruin. Nothing belittles the mind more than the employment of it upon mere fashion: perhaps an embroidered coat or a button on it; a shoestring or a riband; the height of a hat or a cap, or something equally insignificant. Much finery is made in Paris and in other parts of France principally for our market, in the same way as we buy and make beads and other trinkets to send to savage nations. These worthless things first appear among the extravagant people of the cities; the refuse and sweepings are afterward sent to filch the money of our plain country people. Their life is short—perhaps six months or a year in town or country, at the end of which time they are discarded; for nothing is so disgusting in the chameleon eyes of fashion as old finery—and then it may be seen on the backs of servants, as presents from silly masters and mistresses, who are ever complaining of bad service, and who thus debauch the morals and tastes of their menials by the use of that which is entirely unsuitable to their condition."

If we except England, which most nearly resembles us in this respect, the United States is the only country without a national costume. True, the *fashionable* in every European kingdom gratify their folly by perpetual changes in their dress; but the mass of the people are sufficiently independent of them to have a dress of their own, unvarying in its form from generation to generation, so that articles in their wardrobe are often handed down as heirlooms in families. But this love of dress, with its costly changes, pervades every class of our community, from the heiress with her large income, to the menial whose monthly wages scarcely suffice to keep her comfortably clad in the coarsest and cheapest materials. Hence we seldom find among the latter class a disposition to save money, or anything like prudence in its expenditure. Thus, among the multitude of gayly-dressed females on Sundays, who from their appearance might be taken for "ladies", in the fashionable acceptation of the term, there are probably few who, with all their finery, possess such useful articles of apparel as are requisite for health, comfort, and true respectability; and it is almost always the case, that those who make the most show on holydays are the most slatternly and meanest clad on working-days. Females of this description will often expend two or three months' wages upon a fine bonnet or a silk dress, while they have not a pair of common shoes sound enough to keep their feet dry and warm, or sufficient under-clothing to protect them from the severity of the weather; and thus they lay a foundation for future want and misery, by contracting diseases which will incapacitate them for labour, which is their only dependance. There are but few housekeepers in our land that have not had opportunities of noticing the unhappy effects of this love of dress in their servants: a passion not only productive of wretchedness, but too often of crime and the lowest degradation.

Let American mothers, then, commence a reform in their style of dress, not only for their own sakes and for that of their daughters, but for the benefit of those who look up to them for an example, and who are now led into the most serious errors by their influence. Intemperance in dress is fraught with evils no less real, though less apparent, than intemperance in drinking, and is scarcely less debasing to the female mind and character than the passion for strong liquors in the other sex. Economy, simplicity, and a chaste taste should regulate our fashions for female attire, and these will never lead to ostentation or extravagance. When our females are tempted to array themselves in some gaudily-embroidered mantle at a cost of eighty or a hundred dollars, let them content themselves with the simply elegant one that is far less expensive, and remember how many suffering widows and orphans they could comfortably clothe with the amount thus saved. When the shopman displays his costly handkerchief, its fabric scarcely visible through the closely-wrought needlework, and for which he asks a sum sufficient to dry the tears of many who are crying for bread around them, let them reflect that the only use for which this dainty article is intended is to be held between the tips of their fingers as they promenade the city: an ensign proclaiming to all who see it, not only a *wilful waste* of money, but a *woful want* of common sense; and let this consideration save them from the folly of purchasing what is really worse than useless. If in every article of personal attire the less expensive and more tasteful were wisely chosen, how considerable a sum might be saved in a single suit alone; and to what important uses might it be applied. What would be thought of a man who should buy fifteen or twenty barrels of flour, and then empty their contents into the river? Would he not be branded a madman? and would not the curses of the poor be heaped upon his head? And is not the female who throws away upon two or three useless decorations an amount of money sufficient for the purchase of double this amount of food, equally and no less criminally wasteful? By such extravagance no one is really benefited: the merchant realizes probably no larger profits than he would from a useful fabric; the time of the manufacturer is consumed upon what is of no actual value; and to what is all this waste of capital and of labour to be ascribed? To female extravagance: and for this wicked prodigality there must hereafter be a fearful reckoning. How many of the poor and the wretched might be relieved with what is thus squandered upon vanity. Our Saviour has identified himself with the children of poverty and affliction, and He will say to such as have refused to succour them, "Inasmuch as ye did it not to one of the least of these, ye did it not unto me."

The same waste and extravagance are to be seen in the houses and in the whole style of living of those who aspire to be thought fashionable. "The country," says Sedgwick, "is deluged with gewgaws: there is an immense expenditure upon the most frivolous products, for no other reason than—it is the fashion. It is this prodigious passion for finery that makes poor and keeps poor very many among us. Like children, they cover their bodies and fill their houses with bawbles, playthings, and trinkets." Whether it be that the rich in our country, or those aiming to be thought so, are seldom persons of real refinement, we know not; but certain it is, that though we find in many mansions a cumbrous and gaudy excess of ornament, there are very few in which is exhibited anything like correct taste. Instead of that beautiful fitness of proportion between the size of the apartment and its furniture; that harmonious combination of colours so pleasing to the eye of the artist; and that graceful arrangement equally removed from rectangular precision and fashionable disorder, producing a general effect of chaste and simple elegance, we find small-sized rooms crowded with expensive cabinet-work, tables, chairs, lounges, ottomans, and *fauteuils* of various shapes, forms, and hues, the walls glittering with large mirrors, cut-glass lamps and chandeliers, the windows darkened with cumbrous drapery, and the coup d'œil presenting a confused mass of ill-assorted colours, disproportionate forms, and tinsel glare. Their expensiveness gives to these articles their chief beauty in the eye of the fashionable proprietor; and if a fine painting or piece of sculpture happen to be placed among them, because it is fashionable in Europe to purchase such things, the visiter is almost sure to be favoured with an account of its cost, as if its merit were to be graduated solely by the sum paid for it. Few books are to be seen except those employed to decorate the centre-table with the gorgeousness of their bindings; for if by chance an old and valuable library has been inherited from some learned relative, it is either deposited in a lumber closet, or carefully hid from view within the doors of a fashionable bookcase.

Thus we find in our dwellings the same ostentatious extravagance as in our personal decorations; the same useless display, in violation of all the principles of true taste. What immense sums might be saved in furnishing our apartments, were a just taste, instead of show, our criterion. It is disgraceful to us, as a people, to think of the millions wasted in vanity and folly; to reflect that American society, instead of presenting a model of classic simplicity and refinement—a beautiful representation of the unadorned dignity of republican government—is ridiculed, and justly ridiculed, as a servile imitation and ridiculous caricature of European fashions, remarkable chiefly for wasteful extravagance; for it is asserted by one of our own writers, " That travellers and strangers agree that the people of the United States are in many particulars the most wasteful of all civilized people on earth." If the sums thus lavishly thrown away upon trifles were all expended among our own countrymen, it would still be censurable to encourage all this expenditure of time and labour upon bawbles that are worse than useless. But millions upon millions are in this way annually subtracted from our pecuniary means, to fill the treasuries of European kings, or to swell the fortunes of foreign manufacturers. If a hundredth part of these immense sums, thus recklessly wasted, were employed in providing comfortaable dwellings for all our people, in improving our soil, in perfecting the science of agriculture by judicious experiments, and in other objects of real utility, of what incalculable advantage would it be to the community at large. If, again, an inconsiderable portion of it were expended in furnishing the means for cultivating a sound and enlightened public opinion, by establishing free libraries, and promoting public lectures, who can tell the amount of good that would thus be realized? We should then become a reflecting and right-judging people in regard to all the important subjects connected with our individual and national welfare. And for what are all these benefits, public and private, sacrificed? We repeat it—to minister to an inordinate passion for finery and show, and to gratify woman's desire for ostentatious display!

Again, the sums of money lavished upon our fashionable entertainments would form a startling aggregate, could we collect them into one, so as to ascertain the whole amount. The cost of these separately is probably seldom estimated, even by those who give them. Indeed, those addicted to extravagance of any kind rarely keep any record of their expenses. But were this generally done, we should not so often see bankruptcy and ruin following in the train of extravagant living, as there would then be something to give alarm, and to put a check upon the gratification of this passion for show; and were our fashionable dinner and party givers to sit down in every instance and count the cost, it would materially lessen the number of these entertainments. Expensive wines, French confectionery and French dishes, decorations of the rooms, hire of additional servants, pay of musicians, and numerous other items, often swell the expenditures on these occasions to a sum that, with economy and good management, would support the family for several months.

"A woman," says a writer in the N. Y. Evening Post, "cannot prepare one of these evening parties, or a large expensive dinner, without ample funds; and if she undertake it, it must be at the expense of something—dignity, refinement. Let any one who doubts this place himself near the door the day after one of these entertainments. If he were not told that the linen, cut-glass, silver, chairs, and cooking utensils were the property of shopkeepers and neighbours, and were in the act of being returned, he would fancy the family were absconding and cheating some honest creditor, so softly and so cautiously do all the servants creep out of the house with the hidden articles." And for what purpose is all this meanness of shining in borrowed finery? this jackdaw strutting in peacock plumage? this shameful, sinful waste of money? Simply to gratify a love of ostentation—to outshine some fashionable competitor. In such entertainments there is neither hospitality nor social enjoyment; they are got up for the momentary amusement of a motley mass of human beings of different sexes and ages, that they may spend a few hours in eating and drinking, dancing, flirting, or gossiping, amid confused sounds of musical instruments, loud voices, and hurrying footsteps. When the brief show is over, and the gay crowd of triflers has dispersed, leaving the disordered halls desolate and deserted, how can the wearied entertainer forbear asking herself, "What is my reward for all this expenditure of time, money, and labour?" Not a single feeling of rational satisfaction can arise in the heart to afford the slightest remuneration for all this idle and foolish waste. It must be felt to be nothing but "vanity and vexation of spirit."

"In France and Germany," says the writer just quoted, "these evening meetings are the nurseries of the arts and sciences. There men try their strength, and gather together the hints and conjectures which are thrown out, and which, but for this collision of intellect, would be forever lost to science and literature; and there women are welcome guests and critics. Men there want no other gratification than what results from the interchange of mind." And surely neither sex in our own country should require anything more; for they mutually need such opportunities for the cultivation of their minds and the refinement of their tastes. But few of our men are so deeply engaged in abstruse studies as to need relaxation in idle small-talk, if, indeed, even these studies should ever give place to such relaxation. Their days are for the most part spent in amassing wealth, or in the practical details of professional business, and they have then neither opportunity nor leisure for literary or scientific pursuits. How important, then, that their evenings should be devoted to such objects, and that these parties should be made the means of awakening an interest in them? And our women, too, with their pressing domestic engagements, and the necessity of confining their attention so much to the mere physical wants of their families, of what inestimable advantage would such evenings be to them, in elevating their tastes, increasing their knowledge, and fitting them thereby to be better wives and mothers? The spirit of society in all our cities, with the exception, perhaps, of one, is essentially vapid and trifling, so much so as to induce all those who might awaken a better spirit to withdraw from the coteries of fashion, leaving them principally in the possession of giddy girls who have recently "come out," and silly fops, few of whom have yet attained the legal right of assuming the toga of manhood. Is it to be wondered at, then, that vanity and folly should predominate among us, when so many of our youth are thus recklessly launched upon the tide of fashion, without either intellect, age, or experience to guide them? It is these fashionable young men and maidens who afterward become the masters and mistresses of the households of our land; and what better things could we expect than those we see taking place around us?

It is mainly woman's influence which is the cause of "this indifference to what is great, this passion for what is frivolous," so characteristic of a large portion of American society. It is this which has enslaved us to the tyranny of fashion, and this fashion is, in fact, the representative of the "aggregate opinions" of our women; nor can we deny "that the whole comfortless, senseless, heartless system of ostentation is found," if not in woman, "in the education we give her." It is to the education of our females, then, that we must look for the fountain-head of the evils we deplore.

The present system of female education is based upon false principles. In contrasting it in its present state with the narrow circle of acquirements to which it was limited in former times, we are apt to estimate it too favourably. True, woman is not now, as formerly, forbidden access to the temples of science and literature—is not condemned to be without intellectual light and freedom; but is she taught to make a right use of these higher privileges? In one respect she has lost immeasurably by the change: she is no longer domestic; whereas, narrow as was the circle in which the sex were in olden times permitted to move, and few as were their acquirements, yet their sphere was *home*, and their acquirements such as made their highest happiness consist in household duties and in the exercise of the family affections. Unhappily, in enlarging the circle of female accomplishments, we have given our chief attention to those which excite a craving for public admiration and display; and were it not for the force of public opinion in other respects, the course so generally pursued would tend more to train corrupt and brilliant Aspasias and Cleopatras, than noble and virtuous Volumnias and Cornelias. And is it not to be feared that among fashionable women, even in this Christian land, there are fewer examples of moral greatness of character, as wives, mothers, and patriots, than were found among the heathen women of Greece and Rome in their palmy days?

The best system of education for woman is that which will enable her to make the best home. To contribute to the comfort and happiness of domestic life; to purify its pleasures; intellectually and morally to elevate its character; to have, in short, all her dispositions and acquirements so moulded as best to minister to these results —this should be the chief object in female education. But such, it must be admitted even by the least reflecting, is not the end either sought for or attained by our present system. We begin wrong with the female even while an infant in the cradle; and among the first influences exerted are those which tend to foster the seeds of vanity, the most anti-domestic of all the vices. Before the child can speak, its attention is directed to the pretty frock, the gay riband, the golden-clasped necklace, and the lavish adulation and caresses bestowed upon the fairest face in the little group of sisters; and this graves upon its infant heart the indelible lesson that personal decorations and mere external beauty are more to be desired than anything else. The love of admiration and display thus early instilled, is more actively inculcated as she advances to girlhood. Precepts and admonitions are freely imparted, the sole motive of which is to increase and strengthen this love. No principles of independent action are inculcated—such as would prove to her a never-failing source of right conduct in every situation—but she is taught to look to others, and to be governed entirely by their commendation or reproof; thus subjecting her to a rule of guidance constantly varying with associations and circumstances, and leaving her wholly to the control of accidents.

After being thus trained through the first years of life, she is thought to be of sufficient age seriously to *begin* her education, as though that had not been begun years before. The first step, perhaps, is to send her from home; and thus, in her most ductile years, she is altogether withdrawn from those domestic influences which, though impaired in their value by the vanity of the mother, are still, on the whole, more favourable to the feminine character than any she is likely to find in their place under a strange teacher, and among a crowd of strange children. Her little plays, so congenial to her age, and which may be regarded, in many particulars, as a preparatory initiation into domestic duties, are all forbidden her at school, where she is forced to sit unoccupied for many hours in the day, and thus the activity of her spirit and her desire for employment are nipped in the bud. Her heart, too, grows cold and selfish, from being so early deprived of the society of those she loves and by whom she is beloved; while among her new associates she finds little else than an exclusive regard for themselves, and an anxiety to promote their own gratification, though it be at the expense of others. The love of admiration and display which she has brought with her from home receives here a new impulse, from the competition and rivalry systematically encouraged by her teacher, and not less effectually, though more incidentally, by her fellow-pupils. She finds that the approbation of the former is bestowed more on mere natural quickness of parts and a forward display of learning, than on patient, persevering industry, and the retiring modesty of true genius; and by the latter she is taught the omnipotence of fashionable dress in securing the respect and attention which are due only to moral worth and sound mental acquirements. The studies pursued in our fashionable schools are for the most part those which will make the greatest show in the shortest time, and with the least intellectual application. The perishable flowers of a season are more assiduously cultivated than those of slower growth, but more useful and enduring; and subjects which would invigorate and discipline the mental powers are neglected for those of the most trifling nature. The light soil of memory is alone relied upon; while the more slowly-acting but deep and inexhaustible one of thought and reflection is too often left almost wholly untilled.

The acquisition of mere accomplishments, such as music, dancing, and embroidery, usually consumes one half of the period allotted to female instruction, and these scarcely come within the pale of real education. A girl may warble Italian airs with the practised skill of a Malibran, or "play like a professor;" she may dance with all the lightness and grace of a Fanny Elssler, or rival the colouring of Nature's pencil in her elaborate embroidery, and yet be miserably educated: indeed, her very perfection in these accomplishments is, perhaps, the strongest evidence that she is lacking in judicious mental training. One designed to adorn private life, and to fill the responsible station of a daughter, sister, wife, and mother, should devote the precious season of youth to higher objects, and has but little time to waste upon mere accomplishments. Where there is a decided talent for music or drawing, it should to a reasonable extent be encouraged; and a competent knowledge of either, or both, may be acquired without intrenching upon the time that should be devoted to more solid and necessary studies. Both of these may be practised by mothers for the gratification and instruction of their children, and be made delightful additions to home enjoyments. But the art of dancing does not merit the same commendation; for it rarely, if ever, finds a place among the pleasures of the domestic circle. The gay world is the appropriate theatre for its exhibition; and its tendency is to depreciate home-born happiness, and to excite a thirst for public admiration and fashionable amusements.

It is their general anti-domestic tendency which is the greatest defect in our modern systems of female education; and to this we may trace that restless craving for the excitement of public duties and public pleasures, which so strikingly characterizes the aggregate of female society at the present day. Home responsibilities and enjoyments are overlooked, or wantonly deserted for those of a more ostentatious character that are to be found abroad. Thus comparatively few women at the present day are content to be simply useful, and to shine in the domestic circle alone; and this is but the natural result of an education which aims chiefly at attracting observation, and has greater regard to the "praise of men" than to the favour of God.

A fashionable boarding-school, under the most favourable circumstances, is but a miserable preparation for domestic life. Were any one to contrive a system with the design of most successfully forming artificial, worldly women—fashionable automata—merely intended for exhibition, and devoid of every qualification for the serious duties and relations of life, he could not devise a mode better calculated to effect this object than the course of education generally pursued in these establishments. Indeed, the prevailing system of female education is everywhere lamentably defective; and it must be owing to a powerful corrective principle in woman's heart when she is enabled so far to recover from its mischievous effects as honourably to fill the station for which she is designed by her Maker.

Were it not so serious a matter to find the highest interests of the sex thus trifled with, the advertisements of many of our fashionable schools would be a fit subject for ridicule. In addition to the common branches, as Reading, Writing, Arithmetic, Geography, and Grammar, we find History, Natural Philosophy, Chymistry, Botany, Astronomy, Mathematics, Natural Theology, Political Economy; the Greek, Latin, French, and Italian languages; Vocal Music, with instruction on the Harp, Guitar, and Piano; Drawing and Painting of every kind and degree; Bead Work, Chenille Work, Embroidery, making of Fancy Articles, &c., &c.; thus promising to young females the acquisition of all these arts, sciences, and accomplishments during the few years spent at school, when a whole lifetime of close application would prove insufficient for the thorough mastery of many of them. These multifarious acquirements, the catalogue of which is so ostentatiously displayed, are not only promised, but actually attempted; and the simple pupil is flattered and cheated into the belief that she is exceedingly learned and accomplished, while her mind is, in fact, left as barren and uncultivated as the desert heath. Her memory has been loaded with scientific nomenclatures and skeleton abstracts, of the real meaning of which she has, perhaps, scarcely a single definite idea. She is never taught to think, to reason, or to act, and is in reality less wise, after having completed the circle of her learned labours, than is the girl who can neither read nor write, but who, by making the best of her circumstances, has succeeded in training her mind to right thinking, and her heart to right feeling and acting. The sole end of all this verbiage would seem to be, to go through with a parrot-like recitation in the class, or at the quarterly or annual exhibition. Not one of these subjects is, indeed, beyond the reach of the female mind, and most of the sciences might be made interesting and useful even to children, by imparting to them a simple knowledge of the *facts* on which they rest; for *facts* should always precede theories, and intelligent ideas be antecedent to the use of abstract terms or arbitrary classifications. Little more, however, can be done by the best teacher, in the limited period allotted to a course of scholastic instruction, than to lay a foundation and create a *desire for knowledge*, which shall lead to higher acquisitions by the process of self-education. The little that can be effectually taught at school should be real; and no more should be promised than can be performed. But in most of our fashionable schools, it is merely an ostentatious display of pretended acquisitions, where there is not even the semblance of reality. Such a course is enough to turn the most sober head and to stultify the soundest intellect. If even the solid sciences are thus made ministers to a vain show, how much more powerfully must those accomplishments, the direct tendency of which is to create a desire for public display and the applause of the crowd, be exerted in fostering female vanity. Thus the precious seedtime of life is suffered to pass away, nay, to be miserably wasted, without anything that is valuable to the mind or character being sown, and where the only harvest to be expected are the thistles and weeds of self-conceit and folly.

The young lady having arrived at a certain age, is taken from school, and it is said " she has finished her education." Instead of endeavouring to make amends for past neglect, by now instructing her in the knowledge and practice of household duties, and teaching her to love and adorn her home, the next step is to introduce her into society; and by this is meant that she shall be permitted to keep away from home, to spend her mornings in visiting, and her evenings in balls, parties, and places of public amusement. She is taught to exhibit herself to the best advantage, by arraying her person in the most fashionable dress, and seeking every opportunity to show off her accomplishments. The artificial manners in which she has been carefully drilled at her boarding-school are now brought into full display in their appropriate sphere—the world of fashion—and she studies to conceal her natural character and real feelings under the veil of affectation. She finds but little use even for the superficial scientific knowledge she has obtained at school, as music and dancing are the only acquirements for which she has any occasion. She has neither taste nor leisure for mental improvement, for her time and thoughts are wholly engrossed by company, dress, and fashion.

And what is the object of this constantly-repeated routine of daily and nightly exhibition in public? It is to secure a chance for matrimony—that state for whose duties and responsibilities there has not been the slightest preparation from infancy to womanhood. The end so assiduously sought after may, to be sure, be attained; for some brainless fop, or even a man of character and intellect, may be fascinated by the giddy belle, and the partner in a waltz or cotillon may be chosen as a partner for life. Then the sunny days of courtship, and the éclat of the wedding, with its gay paraphernalia of fine dresses and parties, are exactly suited to her fancy and her tastes. But the enchantment all vanishes so soon as the gayeties of the bride must be given up for the duties of the wife and the cares of the manager of the household. It is now that she turns with disgust from the responsibilities resting upon her, and craves the excitement of fashionable life to atone for the dulness of her home. To emancipate herself from the slavery of housekeeping, she often persuades her husband to take apartments at some fashionable hotel or boarding-house, that she may have unrestrained liberty to enter into every kind of fashionable amusement.

In former years, a home was provided for the future bride, to which she was taken as soon as she became a wife; but at the present day, whenever the fortune of the husband is not equal to the extravagant expenditure of an ostentatious establishment, the fashionable married pair make a boarding-house their home; if, indeed, it be allowable to call it by so sacred a name. This practice, now so common in our cities, is fraught with many evils, and strikes at the very root of domestic happiness and the domestic virtues. A woman may thus escape the trials of housekeeping, it is true; but the want of a home, in its proper sense, may be no less fatal to her husband's character than to her own. The generality of men prefer dwelling under their own roof, however humble it may be; and whenever we find a married man at a boarding-house, it is most frequently owing to the choice of the wife. A female with the most vacant mind, if blessed with domestic tastes, will find employment and happiness around her own fireside; and if she be a lodger in the house of another, she must still have occupation, and, not finding it there, she seeks for it abroad. Her husband, too, from constant and intimate association with young men, some of whom, perhaps, are of dissipated habits, may be led to lose all relish for simple domestic enjoyments; and in being deprived of the quiet happiness of his own fireside, he is deprived of the moral influence of home—that salutary preservative against the temptations arising from his daily contact with a selfish, corrupting world. Under such a course of training, need we wonder that so many women are to be found who seem to think that "life is of no use but to make or remodel dresses, and who act as if they were made to be walking-blocks for showing off to advantage the workmanship of the riband and lace manufacturer, of the mantuamaker and the milliner."

Looking to the baneful influences under which she is brought, woman is rather to be pitied than upbraided; for if so large a portion of our females are slaves to show and fashion, and regardless of what is really exalted and great, the cause is to be found in our defective systems of education, and in the senseless and pernicious customs and usages so prevalent in modern society. Woman with us is educated *for the world*, and not for her natural and only appropriate sphere—*domestic life*. The rule of the wise man in respect to her training has been inverted; and, instead of being brought up "in the way she should go," all the influences to which she is subjected tend to turn her from the right course. Her native traits of character, which, by judicious cultivation, may be exalted and refined to answer the noblest purposes, have, by an opposite course, been unnaturally forced into defects. Thus her love of approbation, implanted for the best ends, and so wisely suited to her condition, is fostered into vanity, and her taste for the beautiful perverted into a frivolous passion for finery and display. If her nature prompts her rather *to* follow than to lead, to imitate rather than to invent, is she not wronged by being educated to follow corrupt and fallacious guides, and to be a servile copyist of the worst models? The timidity and reserve which prompt her to shrink from revealing the depths of her heart, and the whole truth of her emotions, are trained into mere affectation and artifice, leading her to seem what she is not, to sacrifice the true to the false, and to study in everything outward effect more than inward principle. By such a course, the distinctive peculiarities of the female character, which, when rightly directed, become the glory of woman, are converted into weaknesses and foibles which constitute her shame. Those who are so ready to seize on the follies of woman as a fitting theme for censure and ridicule, should remember that it is not woman as she came from the hands of her Creator, but woman as education and society have formed her, in whom these follies are found.

Woman was not made to devote her life to vain and frivolous pursuits—not given to man for a toy to amuse his idle hours; but to be, in truth and in reality, a helpmate to him—a minister for good. In undervaluing the character and degrading the condition of woman, man seals his own degradation; for he is subject to her influence from the cradle to the grave; and this influence may be exercised for evil no less powerfully than for good. The aggregate of female mind and character in every country is a faithful index to the mind and character of its men. Man, therefore, is called upon, by every consideration, to do all that is in his power to elevate, both intellectually and morally, the standard of female character, since by this means alone can he ensure his own elevation. And for still stronger reasons should woman labour indefatigably in the same righteous cause. It is *her own cause;* and it is only by so doing that she can acquit herself of her duty to her sex, by fitting it to ascend to its true position in society.

CHAPTER IV.

RELIGIOUS WOMEN.

"Every one has made the observation that there are many more women who are religious than men; but the final cause of this has not so often been remarked. Divine Providence, by this discriminating favour to one sex, pours influence into social fountains. As are the mothers of a nation, so will be the sons, and, in a measure, the husbands."—*Christian Panoply*.

"Do the duty that lies nearest to thee," says the German sage. "Oh! that we could all make this the motto of our heart and of our life, and do the duty that lies nearest to us with all our heart, and all our mind, and all our strength."—*Woman's Mission*.

It is a gratifying subject of reflection to the patriot and the Christian, that so great a number of the women of our country may be included in the religious class. The Christian women of America are designed to be the regenerators of female society; and we look with unwavering faith to their purifying influence, as the means, under God, which is to counteract the widespread corruption of fashionable vanity and folly. Though commanded to come out from the world, and though their tastes and feelings equally withhold them from associating intimately with the fashionable class, yet they possess a weight of influence which makes itself felt even there. The giddiest girl, while flying through the mazes of the dance, or thoughtlessly laughing at the silly or profane jest of some brainless witling, may be suddenly arrested by a conviction of her sin and folly, as the remembrance of a pious mother or sister comes over her thoughts.

In the greater number, and it may perhaps be said, in every society of the present day for the spread of the Gospel, and the moral and religious elevation of man, woman is taking an active part, and has a prominent place assigned to her. If straying lambs are to be gathered into the fold of the Sabbath school; if churches are to be erected in destitute places; if young men are to be educated for the ministry; if the Bible and the missionary are to be sent to the heathen, or to the ignorant and benighted of her own land; or if any benevolent object is to be effected—pious and charitable, in all these undertakings she is called upon zealously to co-operate. She is an efficient agent in the collection of funds, and often the largest amounts cast into the Christian treasury are the fruit of her labours. Her spirit of active benevolence knows no bounds. She will leave her children and her home to look after the charity school or the orphan asylum; to perform the duty of president, secretary, or treasurer in some charitable association; to go from house to house with the printed tract, or the word of spiritual admonition and advice; or to solicit donations for the different societies of the day. Relinquishing the comforts of her own fireside, she will venture forth in the wintry storm, and enter the cold and wretched abodes of poverty, to minister to the wants of the hungry, the naked, and the perishing. And in this great work of doing good—in giving a portion of her substance to the needy; in instructing the ignorant; in seeking, in short, on all occasions, to do what she can in the cause of religion and humanity, woman has ever been a zealous disciple of her Master, from the first promulgation of the Gospel to the present state of diffused Christian light and knowledge. We may trace her footsteps in every path of duty; and even among those who leave their pleasant homes to carry the glad tidings of salvation to the savage sons and daughters of our wilderness, or take their last farewell of their native land to embark upon the trackless ocean, to spread the light of revelation over the moral wastes of Asia or Africa, we see woman—feeble, delicate woman—taking her place as the Gospel pioneer or the Gospel emigrant, strong in faith and undaunted by danger. Thus we find woman ever readily responding to the call for her aid, however arduous the task or distant the field of exertion; and if in some of these labours she may have been led to disregard her more appropriate and imperative duties, she will not lose her reward: the Righteous Judge will look upon the motives of her heart, and pardon her mistakes in action. If her desire to do good has been misdirected, the blame will rest upon those who have sought to lighten their own responsibilities by her assitance, and who, in doing this, have withdrawn her from the duties more directly imposed upon her by her Maker. It is a singular fact, and one deserving of deep consideration, that while the claims for female political rights made by ultra-reformers and social disorganizers have been so justly condemned, as tending to draw woman from her appropriate sphere, she has been urged by others to assume a position in the Church which is liable to the same objection. Many who are strenuous in denying to her all interference in the affairs of the State, are no less zealous in urging her to engage in those of the Church. When any public work of piety or benevolence is to be promoted, addresses are made to the female sex, commending their past efforts in similar services, and stimulating them to renewed exertions. Every argument is brought forward to induce them to labour in adding to the funds to be appropriated to the building of a church, to the education of young ministers, &c.; but when do we hear the Scripture doctrine of home duties enforced? "Let them learn first to show piety at home, and to requite their parents, for that is good and acceptable before God," is a duty as seldom publicly urged upon unmarried females, as is that of being "*keepers at home*" and of "guiding the house," upon wives and the mistresses of families. If, then, these and other similar lessons found on the pages of Holy Writ are left almost wholly untaught, and in their place public services are constantly pressed upon woman's attention, can we wonder at the result? And if her anxiety to do what she can to promote the great interests of humanity has led her into a course of action injurious to her domestic usefulness, it must be admitted that she is not alone to blame.

It is, indeed, deeply to be regretted, that among the many praiseworthy efforts of Christians at the present day, there should be so much in the spirit and character of those efforts that is anti-domestic. Is there not such a thing as religious dissipation, if we may so speak, as well as worldly dissipation? and have not many of our females, by assuming public responsibilities but little in accordance with their nature, and more properly belonging to the other sex, neglected those congenial, paramount, and untransferable duties imposed upon them by the God of Nature and of Revelation? Woman's first duty is to her own family; nor may she leave her home waste and desolate to tend the spiritual vineyard of strangers. If the temporal and eternal interests of her children are ruined by her not training them "up in the way they should go," she cannot expect to escape the condemnation of the Righteous Judge by pointing to those by the wayside whom she believes to have been converted through her efforts, or to the sums collected by her to aid in converting the heathen of distant lands. The mother who fails to fulfil her obligations to those specially committed to her charge, though her name be blazoned abroad in the published records of benevolent or religious associations, and however prominent for Christian zeal she may stand before the world, is guilty before God of having disobeyed his commands; of having violated the law that His own hand has written upon her heart. And the young Christian female, if, in labouring for the public societies of the day, she leaves a toiling, overburdened mother at home to wear out her strength in labours which it is her duty to share in and to lighten, or permits the sick and the indigent, whom she might cheer and assist, to pine in solitude and want, cannot be judged faithful to her most imperative religious obligations. The private duties of filial piety, and of visiting " the fatherless and widows in their affliction," are too often sacrificed for the public services of religious or charitable associations; and if the spirit of the age requires the *latter* to be done, both the letter and spirit of the Gospel command that the *former should not be left undone.*

Next to the obligations which woman owes directly to her God, are those arising from her relation to the family institution. That *home* is her appropriate and appointed sphere of action there cannot be a shadow of doubt; for the dictates of nature are plain and imperative on this subject, and the injunctions given in Scripture no less explicit. Upon this point there is nothing equivocal or doubtful; no passage admitting of an interpretation varying with the judgments or inclinations of those who read. Though St. Paul saw himself the prediction fulfilled, that the spirit of prophecy should be poured out upon " daughters" as well as upon " sons ;" and though his approval of these prophecies is to be inferred from his direction, that those women upon whom the Spirit had been bestowed should have their heads covered while delivering their *inspirations* to the Church, yet even at this very period, with these cases before him, he lays down these authoritative rules : " Let your women keep silence in the churches"—be " keepers at home"—taught " to guide the house." He also commends the faithfulness of the grandmother and mother of Timothy, in having made known to him the Holy Scriptures from his childhood. St. John, also, in his epistle to the elect lady, says, " I rejoiced greatly that I found thy children walking in truth ;" and he does not enjoin upon her to go from home to combat the errors that had crept into the Church, but that she should herself keep the truth, and not receive the deceivers *into her house*, neither bid them " God speed." These intimations of woman's duty are so legible that those " who run may read," and so plain that the least instructed must understand their meaning. And as no female of the present day can be so presumptuous as to suppose herself included in the miraculous *exceptions* mentioned in Scripture, these apostolic injunctions are doubtless to be considered as binding upon all: and if different views have been advocated, and a different practice has in many instances prevailed, the writer of these pages cannot but look upon such views and such practices as in direct violation of the apostle's commands, and as insidiously sapping the very foundations of the family institution.

The family institution is of God's own appointment, and He has ordered it for the best and wisest purposes. In His own Word we find that the spiritual welfare of the family is a paramount object in establishing the marriage relation. It was not for man's benefit alone that a helpmate was given him, and that he was to be the husband of one wife; for the holy prophet declares the revealed will of God when he says, "And did He not make *one*? yet had He the residue of the Spirit. And wherefore *one*? *That He might seek a godly seed.*" The Scriptures are full of express as well as incidental instruction on this point. We read there that the spiritual interests of children are specially committed to the care of parents, and that there is a blessing promised, or a curse denounced, according to their faithfulness or unfaithfulness in this charge. God says of Abraham, "I know him, that he will command *his children* and his *household* after him, and they shall keep the way of the Lord;" and the faithful Joshua declares, "As for me and *my house*, we will serve the Lord." In these examples, their fidelity also as masters is foretold and promised. The example of Eli alone, without mentioning others, will suffice to show that personal piety cannot atone for parental neglect. "In that day," said the Lord to Samuel, "I will perform against Eli all things which I have spoken concerning his *house;* when I begin I will also make an end. For I have told him that I will judge his house forever for the iniquity which he knoweth: because *his sons made themselves vile, and he restrained them not.*" It is not in our power, we know, to give new hearts to our children; yet towards the attainment of this blessing God has assigned us a work to perform, which He has graciously promised to perfect for us. As reasonably might we expect a harvest from the field we have left untilled and unsown, as to look for the fruits of righteousness in our sons and daughters, if we leave them to grow up from youth to maturity without religious instruction. Some pious parents rely upon their prayers for the conversion of their children; but in this we are called upon to labour as well as to pray. Fervent prayer, we may hope, will be answered with a blessing; but, though it is declared that it availeth *much*, it is nowhere said that it availeth *everything*. And on this subject we may repeat the remark of Bishop Sanderson, that "prayer without exertion is presumption, and exertion without prayer is atheism." Both of these are equally enjoined upon us; and the part which God has reserved to himself in the work is to grant his blessing upon our endeavours, in the gift of his Holy Spirit.

Seeing, then, that the family institution is of Divine appointment, and the Holy Scriptures enjoin upon fathers to be faithful as teachers and rulers in causing their households to "keep the way of the Lord;" at the same time requiring of mothers that they be "keepers at home," that by the influence of their presence, example, and instruction they may most effectually promote the welfare of their families, should not all Christian parents honour and cherish this institution far above whatever man has sought out or devised? And they should maintain a jealous watchfulness over the religious movements of the times, lest they be carried away by the spirit of the age contrary to the spirit of the Gospel. The present state of the world, with its stirring appeals, its strong excitements, its public teachings of every kind, and its public occupations and diversions, powerfully tends to depreciate and weaken individual mind and character, and the sacred bonds and responsibilities connected with the domestic relations. By taking a brief survey, therefore, of the state of society, in some of its most prominent characteristics, as it now exists, we shall be the better enabled to judge how far, in following its spirit, even Christian women have deviated from the strict line of duty in regard to their domestic responsibilities.

One of the most striking characteristics of the times is the universality of organized associations, and the high-wrought excitement so frequently produced by them. In these associations, where great numbers assemble together, whatever may be the object intended to be effected, there is a predominating influence which rules all minds, and communicates, as if by contagion, from one to another. When thus uniting in masses, men unconsciously give up their individual opinions, feelings, and judgments, and yield to the voice and the will of those around them. The power of sympathy, so potent in the human breast, makes the nerves of all thrill in unison, every heart throb with the same emotions, and every understanding submit to the same convictions, whether of truth or error, as though one spirit, and heart, and mind animated the whole. Each one is borne hurriedly along by the crowd, and few possess sufficient command over themselves, amid the general excitement, to step aside and calmly observe whither it is tending. These multitudinous gatherings are likened in Scripture to the vast and mighty ocean; their tumult is said to be "like the voice of many waters;" and their excited action may no more be stayed by human opposition, than that of the ocean in its hour of tempest. In such union there is a might which has accomplished widespread desolation and ruin, and glorious achievements too, so strikingly manifesting the power of man that he has been ready to deem himself as God in wisdom and greatness. When man is alone, he can form a just estimate of his strength and his weakness; of what God has enabled him to do, and what is denied to human agency. But when he combines his strength with that of others, and sees mighty results, he is tempted to think himself omnipotent. There was a time when "the whole earth was of one language and of one speech;" and then " they said, Go to, let us build a city, and a tower whose top may reach unto heaven, and let us make a name." "And the Lord said, Behold, the people is one, and they have all one language, and this they begin to do: and now nothing will be restrained from them which they have imagined to do. And the Lord did there, on the plain of Shinar, confound the language of all the earth, that they might not understand one another's speech; and from thence did the Lord scatter them abroad upon the face of all the earth." We too, in our day, have our plains of Shinar, where we build our towers to the glory of man, and the tops of which we would presumptuously raise unto heaven.

A spirit of illiberality, and, if we may so call it, of party exclusiveness, is one of the results of this system of association. It seems not sufficient that we should enter with all our hearts and minds into a particular society, and that we should consider its objects and means better than any other, but we must also believe that it is the only one that has truth or virtue to recommend it. Thus we are so blinded by prejudice as greatly to exaggerate the importance of the end we are seeking to attain, and in the same proportion to depreciate the end sought for by others. If it be particular doctrines or opinions that are to be upheld, we uncharitably conclude that all the truth and all the sincerity are on our side; or if it be a combination of effort for human improvement, or for the overthrow of some prominent vice, we are persuaded that ours is the only way of effecting the object—the only way in which we can hope to elevate our fellow-men above the corruptions of a depraved nature, and ensure that perfectibility of which they are susceptible. We are not only impatient at any opposition, but we cannot endure even neutrality; looking upon all those as being against us who are not actively engaged with us. The spirit of party, though so lamentably violent and all-controlling in our political combinations, is by no means confined to them; it is also to be found more or less in all our associations, whether benevolent, scientific, or religious. Each has its favourite object or its favourite means of promoting it, which it believes to be so much wiser and better than any other, that all must eventually be brought to their way of thinking, and rally around their standard, never for a moment admitting the possibility of a change in their own sentiments, or that their party should embrace the doctrines or principles of another.

As a necessary consequence of this all-pervading spirit of association, there is at the present day a striking deficiency of individual and of private action. Our present schemes for human improvement are of a nature to weaken personal effort, to draw mankind from their homes, and to repress the high and holy influences flowing from our social instincts. The education of our youth must be carried on in *masses*, and hence the crowded schoolroom is deemed the most fitting place for the acquisition of knowledge, and the excitement of competition more favourable to its attainment than the love of it for its own sake, based on the instinctive *desire to know*, so early and so powerfully exhibited in childhood. The student of riper years, instead of trimming his lamp for silent and solitary study, repairs to the public lecture or to the college class; as though these could dispense that sound and available knowledge which is only to be gained by thought and reflection. The duty of charity is performed by societies instead of individuals, and thus it fails of its most beneficent effect, both as it regards the giver and the receiver. Neither men nor women think, feel, or act for themselves, and from this it is that we see so few instances of individual greatness, either moral or intellectual. How rare at the present day are those " master spirits who impart their own activity to human thought, and shed fresh light upon the world ?" Intellectual superiority and soul-freedom never spring forth in giant might but from self-dependant exercise of thought. Men may be personally more free, but their minds they have surrendered to be controlled by others, by the mass, by the omnipotence of public opinion. "Patient thought," which alone made a Newton, is given up for the ephemeral instruction of the public lecturer; and knowledge must be gained with steam-power rapidity, for we cannot wait the slow results of self-education. Hence the superficial character of our current literature: reviews, magazines, and fictitious narratives; picture-books of all kinds, and scenic illustrations for all ages; but how few works of real enduring worth, leading men to think deeply, and think for themselves. We seek to be released as much as possible from the labour of thought, and require our authors to illustrate and explain the truths they would teach as though they were writing for children.

Another distinctive feature of the age, in all

its great movements, whether political or moral, is an impatience for quick returns to our labours, and a constant studying to enlist the passions of the masses, to hurry onward whatever is undertaken. Instead of addressing the reason, and endeavouring to enlighten the judgment by a sober exhibition of truth, some point is seized upon which will best arouse the feelings. Too impatient to wait for the gradual but enduring growth of principle, we call to our aid the more active and impetuous elements of man's nature, that we may realize more sudden and visible results, though these results may be but of momentary duration, quickly forced into maturity, and as rapidly declining into decay. It is not in the pursuit of riches only that men are making so much haste; but the same bustling, hurrying spirit has entered into undertakings whose high ends can only be attained by those who move calmly and steadily forward—their souls filled with a love for all that is great and good, too deep for noisy utterance, and their spirits nerved for every difficulty by the strength of well-considered and abiding principles.

This spirit of association is the great animating principle of all the important movements of the day. Combination of effort has been resorted to, to effect great moral and religious objects, no less than those purely of a worldly nature. All our extensive plans for ameliorating the moral condition of our people at home, and all our missionary operations for extending the light and the blessings of Christianity to heathen lands, have been conducted, and perhaps necessarily conducted, upon this principle. There is danger, however, that in these things, and by this course of action, we may be led to rely too much upon human power. The power of the Gospel is the power of God, and the works to be wrought by it depend more upon the spirit given to man to strengthen him and to fit him for the inculcation of its truths, than upon any combination of human effort, or upon the most munificent donations of Christian benevolence. Still, when we look at the great and glorious results which have followed many of these exertions, we cannot but feel that God has bestowed on them his blessing.

We would not undervalue the good, nor should we overlook the evils either necessarily or incidentally connected with this spirit of association; and we allude to it only for the purpose of showing its effects upon the character and usefulness of woman. Our chief aim throughout these pages is to prove that her domestic duties have a paramount claim over everything else upon her attention—that *home* is her appropriate sphere of action; and that whenever she neglects these duties, or goes out of this sphere of action to mingle in any of the great public movements of the day, she is deserting the station which God and nature have assigned to her. She can operate far more efficiently in promoting the great interests of humanity by supervising her own household than in any other way. Home, if we may so speak, is the cradle of the human race; and it is here the human character is fashioned either for good or for evil. It is the "nursery of the future man and of the undying spirit;" and woman is the nurse and the educator. Over infancy she has almost unlimited sway; and in maturer years she may powerfully counteract the evil influences of the world by the talisman of her strong, enduring love, by her devotedness to those intrusted to her charge, and by those lessons of virtue and of wisdom which are not of the world.

And is not this a sphere wide enough and exalted enough to satisfy her every wish? Whatever may be her gifts or acquirements, here is ample scope for their highest and noblest exercise. If her bosom burns with ardent piety, here she will find hearts to be kindled into devotion, and souls to be saved. Is she a patriot? It is here she can best serve her country, by training up good citizens, just, humane, and enlightened legislators. Has she a highly-cultivated intellect? Let her employ it, then, in leading those young, inquiring minds, which look up to her for guidance, along the pleasant paths of knowledge. Does her spirit burn within her to promote the prosperity of Zion? From this sacred retreat she may send forth a messenger of salvation to preach repentance to a fallen world; a Brainard or a Martyn, to bear the glad tidings of the Gospel to the untutored savage, or to the benighted heathen of other climes. Oh! that the mind of woman were enlightened fully to discern the extent and the importance of her domestic duties—to appreciate her true position in society; for then she would be in no danger of wandering from her proper sphere, or of mistaking the design of her being.

That woman should regard home as her appropriate domain is not only the dictate of religion, but of enlightened human reason. Well-ordered families are the chief security for the permanent peace and prosperity of the state, and such families must be trained up by enlightened female influence acting within its legitimate sphere. Again, there is a tendency in human nature to extremes, in all the changes through which society is passing, from one age to another; and the wisdom of God has devised certain influences to counteract these excesses. The domestic institution, which may be rendered so potential through the properly-directed influence of woman, contains within it a counterbalancing power to regulate and control the passions which give too great an impetus to the social machine. If man's duties lie abroad, woman's duties are within the quiet seclusion of home. If his greatness and power are most strikingly exhibited in associated action upon associated masses, her true greatness and her highest efficiency consist in individual efforts upon individual beings. The religion and the politics of man have their widest sphere in the world without; but the religious zeal and the patriotism of woman are most beneficially and powerfully exerted upon the members of her household. It is in her home that her strength lies; it is here that that gentle influence, which is the secret of her might, is most successfully employed; and this she loses as soon as she descends from her calm height into the world's arena.

Let man, then, retain his proud supremacy in the world's dominion; let him inscribe his name upon its high places, and be the leader of the congregated masses of his fellow-men, with all their excitements, their agitations, and their powerful concentration of effort; but these things belong not to woman. She best consults her happiness, best maintains her dignity, and best fulfils the great object of her being, by keeping alive the sacred flame of piety, patriotism, and universal love to man, upon the domestic altar; and by drawing worshippers around it, to send them forth from thence better citizens, and purer and holier men.

In this age of excitement, it is specially incumbent upon woman to exert her utmost influence, to maintain unimpaired the sacredness and the power of the family institution. "The causes of external excitement," says a late writer,* "are increasing, and along with them the current seems to set from, rather than to, the domestic circle; and parental influences are in danger of being overwhelmed. There are more things out of doors, and fewer things within doors. The right of father, and mother, and home is in danger of becoming obsolete amid the thousand things that are crowding on the minds,

* The author of "Heaven the Model of a Christian Family."

and awakening the wonder, and the enterprise and ambition of the vigorous and the young. It cannot justly excite our astonishment, then, to find the value of home depreciated, its influences weakened, and its restraints less regarded. Sons often seem to look upon the parental abode as the place of mere boarding and lodging; and the opportunities for parental inspection, and the culture of the social feelings which chasten and sweeten life, become circumscribed to the few fleeting moments of a hurried repast. And thus becomes formed a taste for everything abroad and for but little at home. It is for this taste that Satan is ready and diligent to provide, and hence are set on foot shows, convivialities, plays, and entertainments in countless multitudes, to do their part in turning men loose from home, and breaking those hallowed social bonds which are the strong guards of virtue and the firmest barriers to vice. To give these tendencies a more healthful direction, Lyceums, Literary Associations, and kindred institutions have been laudably set on foot; and so far as they are wisely regulated, they tend to impart correctness to public taste, and a more elevated tone to public morals. But while these institutions may be made subservient to great good, they can never prove an equivalent to those hallowed associations of home, the absence of which can never be compensated. And it may also be partially attributed to the same cause, that there has been of late years a remarkable multiplication of religious services, that this awakened public attention that goes so instinctively forth from home for its food and enjoyment, may find provided some healthful spiritual banquets. But it behooves us to guard, lest, while we seek lawfully to accommodate ourselves to these tendencies, we should seem to give them too great sanction. And we are not to overlook that one tendency of these multiplied religious services (we may be allowed to point out their *dangers* without being understood to speak their condemnation) may be to draw attention away from the religious duties of the family—to lessen pious watchfulness and instruction there, and to let down that high tone of sacred importance which should ever attach to the strict religious culture of the family circle.

"Do we behold the family establishment in danger of waning before the excitements of the age? its restraints in danger of being diminished? its hallowed institutions in danger of being overwhelmed? Then there is the louder call upon the fidelity of all who can exert the smallest counteracting influence."

Such is the language of this writer, and such his appeal to those who stand upon the watchtowers of Zion, to give timely notice of the approach of every danger. But may not the same appeal be made with equal force to the religious women of our country? for it is to them chiefly that we must look for aid in elevating the family institution to that high and commanding position in society which will cause it to be honoured and valued as God designed it should be. The Lord God planted this garden, and out of its fruitful soil He will cause all good fruits to spring forth, for those who are faithful in tending and keeping it. In this Eden woman has been placed as a help meet for man; and a work has been given her to do, and pleasures have been given her to be enjoyed, sufficient to retain her a willing resident within its bounds.

Amid the prevailing neglect of household duty, there are, we rejoice to see, some indications of the approach of a brighter day. The awakened interest on the subject of maternal responsibility, which has given rise to our numerous Maternal Associations, will, we trust, be speedily followed by the best and happiest results. And if it has been deemed necessary so far to follow the tendencies of the age as to bring in the spirit of association and of combined action, we still fervently hope that mothers will remember that, though associations may accomplish great things, yet it is only by the individual influence of each one upon her own household that the great end of these associations can be accomplished. The very existence of such associations is, perhaps, the strongest evidence we could have of the lamentable neglect that has prevailed in relation to this matter; for if mothers had studied their Bibles aright, and duly reflected on its directions, they would have needed no farther counsel to instruct them in the duties they owe to their offspring. We would fain hope that these associations are the harbingers of better things to come; that the time is not distant when every American mother shall duly appreciate her domestic responsibilities; and when our homes shall be made attractive by the pure and satisfying enjoyments which religion, intellect, and the social affections have gathered around them. Then, when our husbands and our sons go forth into the busy and turbulent world, we may feel secure that they will walk unhurt amid its snares and temptations. Their hearts will be at home, where their treasure is; and they will rejoice to return to its sanctuary of rest, there to refresh their wearied spirits, and renew their strength for the toils and conflicts of life.

CHAPTER V.

INTELLECTUAL WOMEN.

"The treasures of the female intellect have scarcely begun to be developed. For nearly six thousand years a deep slumber has rested upon the minds of the better part of creation. When the sphere of woman's duties, and the important uses for her intellectual culture are well understood, it will be seen to be in many respects more important that she should have a sound and thorough education than that the other sex should. The intellectual character of the community depends more upon its women than its men; and the influence which they can put forth to elevate the prevailing standard of mind is almost omnipotent."—WINSLOW.

ALTHOUGH the importance of female education is beginning to be more deeply felt, and the attempts towards its improvement have been productive of good, still it may be safely said that the intellectual women of our country are but little indebted for their most valuable attainments to scholastic instruction. They have been, for all efficient purposes, their own educators. Owing to their not having had the advantage of a thorough course of early mental training, there are, perhaps, few among them that can properly be called learned, but there are many possessing great practical intelligence.

In the class of intellectual women we include all those who have identified the knowledge they have acquired, whether from their youthful instructers, from reading, observation, or reflection, with their own minds; who have made it really and truly their own, and practically available for valuable ends—for use, and not for show: women, whose opinions are the result of their own reflection, and not the echo of the opinions of others; whose actions prove them to be rational beings, and not the mere creatures of impulse: women, whose refined tastes, purity of manners, and intelligent conversation show not only that they are gifted with intellect, but that they have been faithful in improving it by cultivation. And we may also properly embrace in this class all those women who think deeply and judge correctly in regard to the various subjects that come within the sphere of their observation and experience; those who possess strong natural powers of mind, but which have been left to their own evolving process amid the circumstances of life; who, though they have never received any instruction from others, nor even been taught, perhaps, to read or write, have, nevertheless, learned to *think*. These last are doubtless to be considered intellectual women, though not in the usual acceptation of the word.

Notwithstanding all the defects in our systems of education, the general female mind has advanced far beyond what it was in former years. Of this there is striking evidence in the question now so strenuously discussed as to the intellectual equality of the sexes. It is not, indeed, now made a subject of contest for the first time; but then, at an earlier period, it was woman who claimed for herself this equality, whereas we now find the other sex no less warmly maintaining it by arguments drawn from facts and experience no less than from reason. This is a point, however, which we shall not attempt to discuss, nor do we see how it can be fairly decided until both sexes shall possess the same intellectual advantages; for individual cases cannot here be relied on to settle the general truth. Nor do we see that any benefit would be gained from such discussion, even were we in possession of the necessary facts to enable us to come to an enlightened decision. Instead of contending about their relative superiority, let it be the ambition of either sex so to cultivate their intellectual powers as to make themselves in the highest possible degree useful in the different spheres allotted to them. An intelligent and highly-educated man, if his moral elevation has kept pace with the progress of his intellect, will always occupy a position in society which will enable him to exert a powerful influence for good. And the woman who to native strength of mind has added the advantages of judicious and thorough culture, and whose character is purified and exalted by religious principle, will in her appropriate sphere be no less honoured and useful. If they shall have both with equal fidelity improved the faculties that have been given to them, and employed them, to the best of their ability, in promoting the great interests of humanity, it is all that will be required of them, and the question as to which nature has been most liberal in her endowments is of comparatively small importance.

But there is an ulterior object had in view in this discussion. Not a few of those who come forward to advocate the mental equality of the sexes, do so in order to show that woman is entitled to the same political rights and privileges as man; a doctrine which, if brought into practical exercise, would tend to the total disorganization of the family institution, and, even more effectually than the spirit of the age, dissolve the domestic ties, and destroy all that makes woman efficient as a moral helpmate of man. But were it even to be proved that woman is man's equal in intellectual capacity, it would only follow from this that a responsibility is resting upon her proportioned to her exalted endowments, and not that she is authorized to relinquish her own appointed sphere of action for that of the other sex. If the great Creator, from whom all our rights, as well as capacities, are derived, has given to woman an influence that is almost without bounds over the mind and morals of the community, He has no less evidently conferred on man the supreme governing power in whatever relates to the external regulations of society.

But, besides the unprofitableness of this controversy, it has been conducted with but little of that calmness and sobriety which characterize an impartial inquiry after truth. There is too much of passion and prejudice mingled in the strife. Ridicule and unfair representation on the one side are answered by recrimination, sarcasm, and false deductions from admitted truths on the other. The opponents of the claims set up in the behalf of woman, instead of entering into a philosophical and scriptural examination of those claims, resort to jests, and witticisms, and unwarranted assumptions. They would seem to shrink from examining the subject fairly, lest they should be drawn to concede more than they wish to do, and to part with some portion of the proud prerogatives they now arrogate as exclusively their own. They can bear "no rival near the throne;" and would rather keep woman a jewelled captive "in a bower of roses"—the passive recipient of man's adulation in his idle hours, than see her elevated to her true position in society as a thinking, responsible being. They have no generous faith in woman; and to prevent her from attaining her true level, they make the absurd and extravagant claims of female disorganizers the ostensible object of their attack, while their real aim is to degrade her intellectually and morally, by striving to persuade her that she is an angel, while they scarcely allow her the possession of reason, and by endeavouring to make her believe that it is her physical attractions alone which bring man in homage to her feet. There are, however, those who are disposed to examine this matter with candour, and with a sincere desire to do justice to woman; and the conclusion to which the wisest and best writers of either sex have arrived is, that the moral and intellectual elevation of society depends chiefly upon the moral and intellectual elevation of our women.

What are human rights? and whence do they emanate, and how are they conferred? They are of two kinds: those proceeding directly from God, bestowed on us as moral and accountable beings by Him, and placing all mankind in a state of equality; and those derived from human laws, and varying according to the civil and political institutions under which men live. No human being, however despotic in power or high in authority, can exercise a lawful dominion over the mind or the conscience. Here God alone is the rightful sovereign, and He delegates his supremacy to no one. In these things we are commanded to call no man master on earth; and our Great Master in Heaven has uttered his condemnation against all those who attempt to lord it over this His rightful heritage. The divine law invests man with freedom of soul, and it is only the supreme Lawgiver himself who can control its internal operations. But with the outward manifestations of these spiritual powers, through the instrumentality of our physical nature, it is different. We are free to think, but not equally free to express our thoughts, if they injuriously affect the interests or the rights of others; and the actions prompted by our freedom of volition are subject to modifications and restrictions, according to the human laws under which, by our external condition, we are placed, or according to their consequences in regard to our fellow-men. This expression and these actions must vary with the rights conferred on us by the laws of the social compact of which we are members, except where those laws are in violation of the primary and inalienable rights which we have derived from our Creator. In regard to civil authority over our outward actions, and the divine authority over our spiritual nature, the Saviour has delivered this command: "Render unto Cæsar the things that be Cæsar's, and unto God the things that be God's."* And the apostles followed out this

* The writer would here remark, that she refers to the distinction between the natural rights which man has received from his Creator and those derived from human institutions, merely for the purpose of illustrating the twofold nature of woman's rights in the marriage relation: first, her inalienable rights as a rational and accountable being; and, secondly, those which belong to her position as a physical being placed under a temporal institution. She has not presumptuously attempted to draw a line of demarcation between "the things that be Cæsar's"

precept of their Master both by enjoining and practising obedience " to the powers that be," while they nobly resisted all infringement upon their natural rights; for when they were commanded by the rulers "not to speak at all, nor teach in the name of Jesus," they indignantly replied, "Whether it be right in the sight of God to hearken unto you more than unto God, judge ye; for we cannot but speak the things which we have seen and heard;" thus upholding the duty of obedience to human law in

and "the things that be God's," or to say how far men may be justified or not in resisting the "powers that be," or in disobeying the laws proceeding from them. The right of resistance and the right of withholding obedience in these things depend upon a variety of circumstances, all of which require to be considered in order to determine whether such right is well founded or not.

We are also to remember that Scripture precepts are not always analogous to political axioms; for our Saviour prescribed no laws for the direct regulation of civil institutions. His kingdom was not of this world. Christianity was not intended to have an immediate relation to human governments, though it was doubtless designed to operate indirectly upon them; and has so operated, in a very powerful manner, as the progress of society has clearly proved. *Religious liberty* has usually been the precursor of *political liberty*. It was Christianity which first awakened in man the feeling of personal liberty—of soul-freedom; and this consciousness of personal rights is the surest guarantee for the establishment of universal rights. It is the soul-freedom of the *individual* that gives assurance of the eventual freedom of the *state*.

things pertaining to civil institutions, but as promptly denying it where that law could have no just authority, and fearlessly asserting their right to freedom of thought and speech in advocating a cause intrusted to them by God himself, destined to confer inestimable benefits upon mankind, and not interfering with any of the rightful claims of human governments.

The relation in which woman stands to man may, for illustration, be regarded as similar to that of the latter to the authority of the civil institutions under which he lives; and God has enjoined upon her a certain obedience to man's authority, reserving to her the right of resistance wherever there is an infringement upon her inalienable rights. As a rational and moral being she is man's equal; but as a physical being she is placed under a system of government wisely suited to the present state of existence. The mind or soul is of no sex. The condition of sex is a distinction that affects not the spiritual nature, and the power vested in one sex over the other is a provision consequent upon the fall, and one adapted to the situation of a fallen race. God formed the first pair in his own moral image, and gave them dominion over the rest of creation. He placed them originally in a state of equality; but upon their disobedience woman was made subject to man, both as a punishment for her share in the transgression, and as a condition best suited to their lapsed state. The necessity of labour was at the same time imposed upon man, and intended to operate in the same twofold manner. So long as both continued sinless, there was no need of this subjection of one to the other; for both, of their own accord, faithfully fulfilled their respective duties; both were equally necessary to each other, and equally and only subject to their Maker. But when sin had introduced the element of disunion, and selfishness had sprung up to create discordant feelings and interests, it became necessary to give authority to one as the governor or head. They had rebelled against the Divine law, and hence human law became necessary.

The supremacy of the husband as the head of the family institution is similar to the supremacy of the governing power in a state, and there is the like obligation to obedience in both. But there is nothing servile or degrading in this. On the contrary, "In making obedience due from the wife to the husband," says Wayland, "it is to be remembered that the act of submission is in every respect as dignified and as lovely as the act of authority; nay, it involves an element of virtue which does not belong to the other. It supposes neither superior excellence nor superior mind in the party that governs, but merely an official relation held for the mutual good of both parties, and of their children." Both stations are equally honourable, and should be equally honoured; and both parties are equally necessary and useful as different members of one body: "the eye cannot say to the hand I have no need of thee; nor again the head to the feet, I have no need of you." Indeed, in this case, also, God hath given "more abundant honour" unto those members "which we think to be less honourable;" for while upon man he has bestowed outward authority combined with physical force, to woman he has given intellectual influence and the power of moral suasion. She is required, therefore, not only to submit to man as her head in the marriage relation, but she must not assume to herself any right of participation with him in the management or control of civil or political affairs. But, though woman is thus denied all distinction of a political nature, whenever she shall enjoy the same advantages of moral and intellectual culture as man (one of the rights still, as a sex, withheld from her), she will exercise a scarcely less powerful influence over the opinions of those around her, and thus, indirectly, an influence over the acts resulting from those opinions.

While we would thus debar woman from all participation in affairs of a political nature, some one of our female aspirants to public distinction may point to the pages of history, and triumphantly cite the reigns of a Semiramis, a Zenobia, an Isabella of Spain, or an Elizabeth of England, as examples of the equal capacity of the female mind for government. If, however, we carefully consider the characters of these sovereigns, it will be found that it was the supremacy of intellect alone which strengthened their accidental authority over others, and directed those works which gave splendour to their reigns. In the Scripture history of the Jews we find only one female who appears to have exercised authority over that nation: Deborah, the judge, the mother, and ruler in Israel. But her authority seems to have been chiefly, if not altogether, of a spiritual nature; for she sat under a palm-tree, and not in the judge's seat, and the power she exercised was purely moral and persuasive, stirring up the people to vindicate their rights. Josephus relates, that when Barak refused to go out against the enemy unless she went with him, Deborah thus addressed him: "Thou, O Barak! deliverest up meanly that authority which God hath given thee into the hand of a woman, and I do not reject it."* So that, if this account be correct, and she did for a while exercise temporal authority, she acknowledges that she received it from Barak, while his was derived directly from God.

But the supremacy thus rightfully belonging to man imposes upon him a fearful responsibility. It is liable to be, and, as the history of every age abundantly testifies, has been, dreadfully abused. Among savage nations it has crushed woman into a slave and a beast of burden, while among those not entirely barbarous it has reduced her to a condition no less degrading, as the mere captive and toy of man, destitute of mind, and denied a soul! And if in civilized communities she is exempt from this extreme of oppression, she is far from enjoying the equal rights and protection that are her due. Unjust laws, prejudiced opinions, and tyrannical usages entail upon her, even here, a fearful amount of suffering. Let any one consider the numerous disabilities to which she is subject; the impositions to which she is obliged to submit; or her ill-requited labour,

* Whiston's translation.

where she is compelled to work for her own support or for that of her helpless offspring: let him listen to her tale of misery, of oppression, and of wrong, and it will be seen that even civilized communities are sadly wanting in justice to woman. But who can estimate the amount of suffering, uncomplained of and unredressed, inflicted upon woman through the abuse of man's power in Christian lands? How many females have seen their own hard earnings, upon which their children depended for bread, seized upon by an intemperate husband, to be squandered in brutal excesses, without the power or the right to withhold them from his grasp! And how many a distracted mother has been obliged to steal away her own child and secrete it, to save it from being ruined by its debased and unprincipled father, without the possibility of establishing any available claim to its guardianship, except by having recourse to a tedious and uncertain legal process which she may not have the means to carry through! Many flagrant instances of injustice growing out of the laws in relation to this matter have been brought to the notice of our tribunals; and recent decisions afford a cheering indication that the spirit of equity is becoming more powerful than the mere letter of the law in determining a mother's rights. It is to this gradual awakening to a sense of justice and a more enlightened public opinion that we look with confidence for the redress of woman's wrongs.

Here, then, is a field abundantly ample for the exercise of the highest talents in the defence of woman's rights—to redress her wrongs, and procure her release from the unjust disabilities which now weigh so heavily upon her—without resorting to the indefensible and extravagant claim of political privileges. The relics of darker ages and the customs of barbarism are still found among us. In the higher classes, refinement and the force of public opinion check the manifestation of the spirit of tyranny; but among the ignorant and uneducated, the idea that a husband has a right to treat his wife as a slave is still by no means uncommon. "The tendency to Orientalism" is visible, too, in the false position in which woman is placed, as a being formed for no higher purpose than to be decorated, admired, and valued for her personal charms. Do we not see females in every fashionable circle who fill no loftier station in social life, and who live as idly and as uselessly as the gorgeously-attired inmates of the harem? They have a greater latitude allowed them in regard to personal liberty and their choice of amusements, but their minds are left almost as vacant, and their pursuits are almost as childish and trifling. This false position is not only upheld by many of our customs and habits, but has even been defended by public speakers; and when we hear it said that woman should be kept "like a jewel in a casket," and listen to the soft flatteries and the false adulation offered to her, which so often form the concluding paragraphs of orations and lectures addressed to the two sexes, we cannot help feeling the injustice that is done her. This prevailing system of acted, spoken, and written flattery tends as directly to degrade woman from her true position, as a being upon whom there rests high and solemn responsibilities to her God and to society, as any of the barbarous customs of heathenism.

De Tocqueville remarks, that "in Europe a certain degree of contempt lurks even in the flattery which men lavish upon women. In the United States men seldom compliment women, but they daily show how much they esteem them." He might have found this so in particular instances, but it is by no means universally so; for the European usage is still quite too common among us. Even addresses to promote benevolent objects are not free from this erroneous practice; for in these woman is stimulated to greater activity in her charitable labours by flattery, and by exciting a spirit of vainglorious emulation which has no foundation in Christian principle; and too often the goodness of the end to be attained is alone regarded, without considering whether the means are equally commendable. Nor can we hope for the speedy advancement of the female mind until women are no longer treated as spoiled children—until they are addressed faithfully and honestly, as they ought to be.

If the spirit of Quixotism which has led some of the intellectual women of both hemispheres into a combat against fancied wrongs and political disabilities had been but a spirit of true and noble knight-errantry, seeking to vindicate the just and undeniable claims of their sex, there would have been now a bright prospect of better things in store for them. One of the flagrant wrongs inflicted by society on woman is the erecting a false standard of female character, and suiting her education to it. And in asserting her right to a thorough and judicious training for her high responsibilities; in enlightening public opinion in relation to her true character and position; in endeavouring to remove the discouragements which now press so heavily upon every species of female labour, and in extending its sphere to various occupations now denied to her by selfishness or prejudice: in doing this, and in advocating every other just claim of the sex, there is work enough for the most active reformer, and of a nature sufficiently elevated for the most gifted pen, or the highest moral energy that can be awakened by the spirit of humanity.

The great error committed by the advocates of woman's rights has been, that they have been looking to legislation for that redress which can be obtained only through an enlightened state of public opinion; and, as a preliminary step to this, they have insisted upon the right of suffrage, according to the political maxim that "governments derive their just powers from the consent of the governed;" thus falsely supposing it is only by a direct representation of her own interests that she can hope to have justice done her. But there is no more necessity of female representation for the security and protection of female interests, than there is that each separate trade or pursuit in the community should be specially represented. The most efficient security for the interests of all is that enlightened sense of justice which is ever ready to acknowledge and grant the rights of all. It is not to female voters, female legislators, or female governors, therefore, that we must look for the establishment of woman's rights, but to the force of enlightened public opinion. Nor can anything but the moral and intellectual elevation of her sex bring public opinion to a just appreciation of what position rightly belongs to woman in society; and could she be freed from every fetter that has degraded and every wrong that has oppressed her; could she once attain that elevated station so important to the highest welfare of mankind, no true female heart would sigh for political distinction while standing upon that summit of the social edifice, where she would find enough to engage her warmest affections, and ample scope for the exercise of all her energies.

But, to fulfil the great purposes of her being, woman must be efficiently educated; for, if her intellect be not properly cultivated in early life, the married state, with all its cares and responsibilities, affords but little leisure to commence so important a work, though she may find many opportunities to continue it if a suitable foundation has been previously laid. Man may in some measure correct the errors and supply the deficiencies in his early training by the instruction he is constantly receiving from his intercourse with the world; but if a woman has no intellectual tastes, the routine of her household duties will absorb all her attention, to the utter neglect of mental pursuits. That this subject, notwithstanding all that has been urged in relation to its importance, is not yet appreciated as it should be, is evident from our witnessing no greater results. Communities, as well as "nations, are slow and reluctant learners;" and although upon this matter there has been given line upon line, and precept upon precept, for many years, still the intellectual advancement of woman is far from receiving the attention it so imperatively demands. "A simple question," says Aimè Martin, "will place this subject in a stronger light: Are women qualified to educate men? If they are not, no available progress has been made." Let us apply this question to ourselves: Are *American* women qualified to educate the future men of our country? If they are not, then they are not educated as they should be.

Education, to be of any real value, must be so conducted as to enlarge and elevate the mind, and to lead to practical results; or else all the acquirements made are but useless mental lumber. The ability to read, for example, is only valuable as it may be judiciously applied to the acquisition of useful knowledge; while it may either be suffered to remain inactive, or be employed only to pernicious ends. It is the key which opens to us the vast storehouse of intellectual treasures of every kind; but among these there is deadly poison as well as healthful nutriment; filthy dross as well as pure gold; and "trifles light as air" no less than things most precious. Here is to be found truth in its sober hue and unadorned simplicity, and here, too, is the serpent error, insidiously tempting the eye with its gorgeous colours. We hold in our hand the key, and may enter in; but how much depends upon the wisdom or folly of our choice, and how great is our danger of choosing wrong, unless we have been previously instructed how to choose right.

The books we read have as powerful an influence for good or for evil as the associates with whom we hold daily companionship, and the character of the general mind of a country may be estimated by the character of its popular literature. Applying this test, then, to our own country, what judgment shall we form of its aggregate intellectual condition? We speak more particularly of the female mind.

What are the books most eagerly sought for, and what is the character of the periodical literature specially intended for female use, and exclusively courting female patronage? Although the general taste for novel-reading has evidently declined, yet the "last new novel" is still as attractive as ever to many female readers, though novels of the present day are widely different from what they once were; and the trite question, "Have you read Bulwer's last?" calls forth an expression of sentiments very unlike those suggested by the works of Sir Walter Scott or Miss Edgeworth, and sentiments, too, not the most favourable to female purity. Looking over the periodicals designed for females, we find two prominent characteristics which appear to be considered indispensable in order to secure their patronage: a coloured plate of the fashions, and a plentiful supply of fictitious narratives. The literary portion is suited to the pictorial; and in both, instead of the plain, useful garb of truth, we are presented with the furbelowed costumes of fashionable life. We do sometimes, it is true, find articles of a higher character. But if, to secure readers and a sufficient support, it is really necessary to make ladies' periodicals such as they are, we can conceive of no more cutting sarcasm on the prevailing literary taste of our women. The fault, however, lies not with those who conduct these periodicals, but with those who encourage them. As soon as there is a demand for a more healthful literature from those who cater for the public taste, it will be provided. Still, there are now a few periodical publications for females which are unexceptionable in their character: we allude particularly to " The Mother's Magazine," " The Mother's Monthly Journal," and the " Ladies' Repository," recently established at Cincinnati. The two former are intended for a special object, and this is faithfully kept in view. The latter, which is more miscellaneous, is the only one of its kind in which fictitious narratives are wholly excluded.

But there are other evidences among us indicating that we may look for better things. Books of a more useful and substantial kind than novels are beginning to be written and to be read. Miss Sedgwick has given up the pleasant trifles which formerly employed her pen, and has presented us with several works distinguished by sound sense, and of a strictly practical character. Mrs. Sigourney has laid aside the poet's lyre, whose tones struck so sweetly upon the ear, and has engaged heart and soul in the moral and intellectual elevation of her sex, proving that she can instruct as well as charm. Her "Letters to Young Ladies," and her "Letters to Mothers," are invaluable. The minds of both sexes have been injured by the stimulus of fictitious works. There is everywhere in the human mind a healthful craving for the substantial aliment of truth, where its natural appetite has not been destroyed by improper diet. Happily, the public taste in regard to fictitious writings is undergoing a change: their excess has produced satiety; fewer of such works are published, and they have fewer readers. A more healthful literature, we may hope, will succeed; and we trust the female portion of our reading public will share largely in this reaction. An English writer has said "that there are many readers among American women, but that *thinkers* are rare." The time is near at hand, we hope, when there will be no ground for this reproach; when our women will show that they can think as well as read. The same remark has been applied by another European writer to the men of our country; and the want of original character—of nationality in our native literature, has been frequently alleged against us. We certainly have some original writers, but nothing that can claim to be considered a national literature. In the literature of England we found " a model which accorded with the ideas and habits" still prevalent among us; and, as Madame De Staël remarks, "wherever this is the case, the mind is more inclined to adopt than to create. Necessity alone can produce invention." Our political writers, indeed, found no model in the political writings of England, the principles advanced in them being opposed to the genius of our government; and necessity has given to us something like a national political literature. But not so with the polite literature of England: that we found in many respects so much in accordance with our manners and sentiments, that we adopted it as our own. Still, there is even in this a great deal which is unsuited to us as republicans, and which operates unfavourably upon our national character. We need a literature truly and properly our own — one in conformity with our government and social institutions: a literature exposing the folly and the inconsistency of the anti-republican fashions, tastes, and opinions which we have derived from the literature and manners of the Old World. Our authors should unite in building up a social fabric, the proportions of which shall all be in perfect keeping with the simple majesty of the Doric Temple we have reared to liberty and equal rights.

To the literary females of our country a mission of the deepest interest is intrusted. It is for them to elevate the intellectual character of their sex; to make them truly republican women; to endeavour to provide for them a sound, healthful, and invigorating literature, adapted to their condition as the daughters of this great and free nation. Let them come forward, then, to the noble task of instructing their countrywomen in the high duties which pertain to them; and, above all things, let them be teachers of truth and reality.

But, if fictitious writings cannot be wholly dispensed with, let our works of this kind be at least American. Let no woman of genius among us so far abuse the gifts bestowed upon her as to furnish additional incentives to the already inordinate desire for wealth and luxury, by high-wrought descriptions of fashionable life, with its splendid mansions gorgeously furnished, and their richly-attired inmates; but draw her models from our humble or our truly refined homes; in short, from our genuine American women. Fashionable society in all countries possesses the same general characteristics, and we must look elsewhere for original national character. And in our national female character there is a rich mine for our writers as yet unexplored, which will amply reward all who seek for its virgin ore. It was not the genius of Scott which invented a "Jeanie Deans," but it was the character of the real Jeanie that gave power to his pen. Nothing that is original or morally great is to be found among our artificial women of fashion; they are but faded and worn-out copies of foreign pictures. But among our wives and daughters, who are the blessing and ornament of their retired and unpretending homes, we may discover many a "Jeanie Deans," strong in moral energy and in self-denying affection, and exalted by every virtue that gives dignity and worth to female character. Look at the fairest belle in the coteries of fashion; listen to her stereotyped phrases upon the commonplace topics of the day; her stale repetitions of the sayings of others; her soft nothings, so full of affectation, and then say if you can discover in all this either heart or mind. But turn from her to some humble seamstress, whose daylight and midnight task it has been, perhaps, to prepare the habiliments in which this butterfly devotee of idle pleasure is arrayed, and learn from her the instructive history of the vicissitudes she has experienced. The trials of life have taught her wisdom, and its sufferings have given depth and intensity to her feelings. There is both mind and heart here; and from their inmost recesses she will unfold such pure and lofty truths as are never heard from the giddy triflers of fashionable life, and which could not even be appreciated by them. In eliciting the hidden stores of thought and feeling shut up in the heart of many a woman in humble life, we shall be surprised by beautiful revelations of character, more full of originality and deep interest than are to be found in the creations of the most gifted genius. If our writers would exhibit models of genuine refinement, and of simple, graceful elegance, let them study that domestic circle where, by the intellectual elevation of the mother and her daughters, home is made so lovely and attractive as to take from the gayeties of fashion all their fascination; where cultivated intellect and taste, and pure, unaffected feeling, communicate an indescribable charm to manners and conversation; and where piety sheds its crowning grace over all, giving to the natural character a spiritual life, holier and brighter than aught that belongs to earth. It is from studying life in its humbler and less obtrusive forms—in the experience of the solitary female orphan, thrown upon the world to struggle unaided amid its difficulties and temptations, and triumphing over them all by her unconquerable rectitude and energy; in the struggles of the widowed mother to raise her children above the miseries of want, and to provide for their future advancement by the advantages of mental culture; in the trials of the much-enduring, neglected, and oppressed wife of the brutal inebriate: it is from such sources as these that we can best learn the character of woman in all its moral strength, intellectual force, and unyielding purity.

If there are those who sneer at female virtue in humble life, we will say to such that they are as ignorant of, as they are incapable of appreciating or understanding, the female character. Opinions so disgraceful recoil upon themselves, and inflict no wound upon those they are designed to injure. The examples to be seen of female purity in humble life might well cause many a fashionable woman to feel painfully conscious of her own inferiority. Indeed, fashionable life is more dangerous to female purity than the bitterest privations of poverty; and if the *on dits* tolerated in fashionable society have caused our ears to tingle, and our cheeks to blush with shame for some who are among us, yet we cannot feel they are of us; we look upon them as aliens to our land, as the would-be imitators of a corrupt foreign aristocracy. But our own true *American* women—whatever may be their position in life, whether they are the wives and daughters of our mechanics and labourers, or of our eminent men in high civil or professional callings—it is they who are the worthy daughters of the Republic; and of such we may be justly proud.

Let our women of genius, then, draw their models from these bright examples, and strive to elevate the general female character in our country to the highest possible standard. And our intellectual women—for many such there are who have no ambition to appear as authors, but who can do much by their conversation and example—let them also join their efforts in the great work of female improvement. As they have themselves experienced the advantages of intellectual culture, let them strive to have them extended to all their sex. They should consent to no male monopoly here. There is no study which can give vigour to the mind from which woman should be debarred. If knowledge is power, knowledge will give efficiency to female influence. But let this important truth never be lost sight of, that it is not literary or scientific attainments, of themselves and alone, which can give true intellectual elevation. Women must be made to think—to acquire wisdom as well as knowledge; and wisdom is the result of deep, patient, untiring reflection. If they possess not wisdom as well as knowledge, they will have no better claim to be considered intellectual women than the lettered volume, which is but the inanimate record of the thoughts of others.

Woman is called upon to labour in the cause of female improvement, not only because she owes it to her own sex, but to man and to her country. The prosperity and the decline of nations depend in no small degree upon female influence, according as it is employed for good or for evil. "Descent into ruin," it has been said, "is usually commenced with the false education, the indolence, and the luxurious habits of the female sex." Of what incalculable importance is it, then, that female education be well understood and faithfully attended to. We trust the day is not distant when this education, in its best and most comprehensive sense, shall be extended over the length and breadth of our land; and when that period shall happily arrive, the intellectual women of our country will form a noble phalanx, no less able than ready to promote the highest interests, not of their sex alone, but of society at large and of their country; and be the moral guardians, not only of our homes, but of our Republic.

CHAPTER VI.

OF WOMEN WHO ARE MORALLY GREAT.

"What can a woman be or do without bravery? Has she not to struggle with the toils and difficulties that must follow upon the mere possession of a mind? Must she not face physical and moral pain—physical and moral danger? Is there a day of her life in which there are not conflicts where no one can help her? perilous work to be done in which she can have neither sympathy nor aid? Let her lean upon man as much as she will, how much is it that he can do for her? from how much can he protect her?"—H. MARTINEAU.

"Upon thy heart's own courage call,
On thy immortal hopes rely,
And turn to *Him*, whose love to all
In sorrow's hour is ever nigh."—*Dem. Review.*

MORAL greatness has been, in all ages and in both sexes, a rare attainment; so rare that the examples to be found in the pages of history stand but here and there, in solitary grandeur, and the few who possess it in contemporary society are too strikingly individual to admit a classification. It is from individual instances alone, therefore, that we can draw our illustrations to show what is meant by moral greatness. The Edinburgh Review, in noticing the Memoirs of Mrs. Hutchinson, and paying a just tribute to her memory, makes the following remarks: "Education is certainly far more equally diffused in our days, and accomplishments infinitely more common; but the perusal of this volume has taught us to doubt whether the better sort of women were not fashioned of old by a purer and more exalted standard, and whether the most eminent females of the present day would not appear to disadvantage by the side of Mrs. Hutchinson. There is something in the domestic virtue, and calm, commanding mind of this English matron, that makes the Corinnes and Helioses appear very insignificant. We may safely venture to assert, that a nation which produces many such wives and mothers as Mrs. Lucy Hutchinson must be both great and happy."

The records of English history stand pre-eminent above those of other nations in the moral elevation of its distinguished women. The magnanimous and energetic qualities of the Anglo-Saxon character are no less distinctly marked in that of the women of England than of its men; and the position of the sex among the barbarians of the North more nearly resembled that assigned them by Christianity, than the slavery and privation of character, the state of nonentity, so to speak, to which they were reduced by the tyranny of Southern barbarism, or by sensual corruption and luxurious indolence among the later Greeks and Romans. By the Anglo-Saxons and their descendants women were respected; and this taught them to respect themselves. It was this feeling of self-respect, this self-reliance, "the calm, commanding mind," which gave to the English matrons of other days their moral greatness. They were the counsellors of patriots and statesmen; the trusted repositories of state secrets; the guardians and defenders of the honour and integrity of their husbands; the sharers of their toils and dangers; and, at the same time, the most striking models of domestic usefulness, feminine submission, and devoted affection. England can boast of a Mrs. Hutchinson, a Lady Russel, and many others of like character; but a modern Sappho, Aspasia, or Cleopatra are nowhere found in her annals. The society of her great women was not courted by philosophers, heroes, and statesmen, in hours of idle leisure, for the fascinating elegance of their conversation, their luxurious accomplishments, or the blandishments of their coquetry; but these noble women were sought in domestic privacy for aid and counsel in the hour of their country's danger. They were helpmates in truth and in reality—strong to suffer hardship and to endure adversity for those they loved, and ever ready to protect and succour all who appealed to them in a time of need; but in their virtuous indignation they would have scorned the man who should have presumed to look upon them as mere objects for pastime in an idle hour.

Although the education received by Mrs. Hutchinson, Lady Jane Grey, and other great women of England, was of that wise, judicious, and elevated character calculated to form an enlightened mind, richly stored with knowledge, yet their *moral greatness* was independent of their intellectual training, as is evident from the example of Lady Russel and others, whose literary attainments were but little beyond those of the generality of females at the period in which they lived. It was the education of circumstances, the position in which they were placed, and the depth and intensity of their piety and of their domestic affections, which gave to them that moral sublimity of character that made them great. They sought not the admiration of society, like the intellectual and accomplished De Staël; for home was the scene where their happiness centred, and the love and respect of their husbands and children were the only tribute they either expected or desired. When they went forth from the sacred retirement of domestic life, it was not to shine in the coteries of the fashionable or of the literary, but to *act* greatly and nobly for those they loved, or to promote some object of utility or of mercy. Though a life of seclusion was their choice, yet they shrank not from publicity when duty called them abroad. In whatever situation they might be placed, they were the same; and their elevated character, commanding minds, and calm, dignified self-possession secured for them universal respect and homage, as well in the midst of the tumultuous assemblage, or of a corrupt court, as in the private circle.

Among the eminent women of France, there has been one at a recent period who in moral greatness closely resembled those of England —the unfortunate Madame Roland. Had this female martyr possessed the piety of Mrs. Hutchinson or of Lady Russel, she would have presented the loftiest example of moral grandeur in woman that is recorded in history. Whoever has studied the character of Madame Roland and that of Madame De Staël—contemporary with each other, and both equally celebrated—cannot have failed to observe in their different traits the marked distinction there is between intellectual and moral greatness. The brilliant De Staël was naturally fond of admiration: this, indeed, was her ruling passion; and in her it was stimulated to its extreme point—a craving, restless vanity; while the manifestations of Madame Roland's character were those proceeding from the combined activity of pride and firmness, producing a calm consciousness of power (which she was content to exercise in retirement) and a steady consistency of conduct, the result of fixed principles. There was no moral repose about Madame De Staël; and high as was her own estimate of her talents, she was impatient for the commendation of others, that she might be still more strongly convinced of the superiority of her intellectual endowments. She could not, therefore, be happy without the incense of adulation so lavishly offered to her in Parisian society.

This celebrated daughter of a no less celebrated father, accustomed from infancy to womanhood to the excitement of flattery, and to the admiration of the crowd, found the domestic circle dull and spiritless; while Madame Roland voluntarily relinquished the gayeties of life, and devoted herself to the duties of home and the education of her child. She assisted her husband in his literary labours; and was not only his secretary and amanuensis, but composed many of the papers that were ascribed to him; and, being wholly free from intellectual vanity, she cheerfully surrendered to another all the credit she might have derived from them. What nobleness of soul does she manifest in these sentiments: "If," said she, "my compositions could be of use, it afforded me greater pleasure than it would have done to be known as their author. I am avaricious of happiness, but I do not stand in need of glory." Feelings like these evince true moral greatness, and are peculiarly suited to woman. Let man go forth into the world's arena, there achieve his triumphs, and with proud satisfaction receive his well-earned meed of fame; but what is there in fame to satisfy the heart of woman? Her social position forbids the love of glory, and she stands not in need of it. It belongs to her to labour for good in her appropriate sphere for the sake of the good itself, seeking for no higher earthly reward than an approving conscience, and shrinking from applause as derogatory to the true dignity of her sex, and painful to her feelings as a woman. She should aim at that moral elevation which will lead her to experience the highest gratification in the work she has in hand, without a wish to draw attention upon herself. It was woman's privilege, and not her wrong, to have been "Priestess, Prophetess, the Oracle of the Tripod, the shrouded teacher of the Academy, and the martyr or missionary of a spiritual truth."[*] And is it not now cause for gratulation, and not for complaint, that she can send forth her lessons of wisdom while she herself is unseen? that she can, "in all moral impulsions," lend her aid without exposure to the public gaze? What would she gain by quitting the sanctuary of her home to stand in the pulpit or the forum? Would she not give up all that makes her valuable as woman, without obtaining a single advantage in exchange? It is her true greatness to be content with doing good, without a wish to find it fame; and she should deem it her highest glory also.

Moral greatness is based upon strength and energy of character, and is exhibited in a strenuous and unwavering devotion to some

---

[*] Lady Morgan's "Woman and her Master."

noble end, without any alloy of ostentation or self-seeking. The objects for the exercise of this exalted quality are infinitely varied, and the feelings which call it into action may be very different in different individuals; but it is the same power which carries them forward in their course. In Mrs. Hutchinson and Lady Russel the fame and interest of their husbands were the objects, and conjugal affection the emotion, which quickened their inherent moral greatness into lively exercise. In Madame Roland, it was love of country which fired her heart, and an ardent desire to rescue her crushed and down-trodden countrymen from the grasp of tyranny, which called into activity all the energies of her nature. She worshipped her husband as the impersonation of those principles of liberty and justice to which she had been devoted from childhood. Still, she did not so far forget her dignity or her station as to exhibit herself in the light of a public political reformer; but, true to her sex, she still lived in retirement, and was content to speak and act through her husband. When seated in the midst of the political agitators of the day, she listened with intense interest to their discussions of the great question of human rights, and was fully capable of understanding and of appreciating all that she heard; *but she kept silence,* while she treasured up and pondered in her heart all that was said. When, however, she came to be alone with her husband, she then entered freely and fully into all the plans he so unreservedly communicated to her for the enfranchisement of the people, aiding him alike by her counsels and her pen. If at length she was drawn forth from her seclusion, it was not to make a public show of her zeal in the cause so precious to her heart, but to defend and rescue her husband. It was for him she sacrificed her feelings and her choice as woman; and, whatever may have been falsely alleged against her to cover the iniquity of her imprisonment and death, it was as the *wife of Roland* that she was brought to the scaffold: she paid with her own life for having saved that of her husband. Her moral greatness did not forsake her in her hour of extremest trial. After her condemnation and at her execution, she retained all her tranquillity, firmness, courage, and self-possession. Thus she lived, and thus died—a model of female magnanimity; and however much we may lament that, amid the superstitions which disturbed the faith of her childhood, and the insidious dogmas of the infidel philosophy to which she lent a reluctant ear in her womanhood, she found not the highest source of moral greatness—trust in the glorious truths brought to light in the Gospel—yet in her aspirations to that Supreme Being whose wisdom, power, and goodness her heart ever acknowledged (though to her, alas! an "unknown God"), there were evidences of an instinctive devotion, which, under better influences, might have been expanded into a pure and elevated piety.

Our own beloved country would be found rich in examples of female moral greatness could they be drawn forth from the obscurity which rests upon them. Were we able to trace the lives of the females of our Revolution—a period which "tried the souls" of women as well as men—we could present many a name which would rival in lustre those of the great women of other lands. But, though we are prevented from doing this, as there is no record of their heroic self-devotion, we know that the women of America in those times were ready to submit to every sacrifice in the great cause of their country's independence.

Among the admirable women of that day, none stands forth so pre-eminent in our history, as a model of female moral greatness, as Mary, the mother of Washington. Though there were but few striking incidents in her life, and though her separate biography is yet to be written, still, from the little we know of her, we are at no loss to discover that her character presents one of the purest and noblest examples of moral elevation. It was the simple majesty of her moral greatness which called forth the following remark from certain foreign officers on retiring from her society: "It is not surprising that America should produce great men, since she can boast of such mothers." The highest possible exemplification of that mother's greatness is found in her illustrious son; and she, to whose forming hand is to be ascribed so noble a work, needs no written biography: it is traced in lines of light in his peerless character.

In looking abroad on female society at the present day, we discover but few who have attained a high degree of moral greatness. Neither the circumstances by which woman is surrounded, nor the education she receives, are favourable to the development of energy of character. She in too many instances occupies a position in which she considers herself relieved from the duties which nature and religion have imposed upon her, while her intellectual and physical training tend to incapacitate her for their performance. The customs of society no longer require from her physical labour, except when it is necessary for subsistence; and, wherever she has man to depend on, she is left to a life of indolent leisure. The natural result of this is, that her powers not being called into exercise, she becomes enfeebled in mind and body, and shrinks with a faint heart from everything like toil, difficulty, or responsibility. Thus many of our females are heard to complain of the fatigues attendant on housekeeping, though they may be wholly exempt from any share in its manual labours, while they sigh for the entire freedom from care that is to be found at the boarding-house, where they can escape even from the necessity of *superintending* their domestic affairs. The attention required by their children, and even their continual presence, are a task and a weariness to which they pretend to be unequal: it is too much for them to bear; and, accordingly, the little creatures must be confined to an upper room, with a hired nurse, in their infancy; and, as soon as they are old enough to rebel against this imprisonment, they are sent away from the house, to be kept equally debarred from fresh air and the free exercise of their limbs by being shut up within the walls of a schoolroom. It is wholly forgotten that liberty is one of the rights of childhood, and that all unnecessary restraints upon its exercise will be no less fatal to their intellectual than their physical health in after life. In place of the mother's care, there is the hired attention of the stranger; as though money could purchase a substitute for the self-denying affection of maternity!

And even among those mothers who do not thus neglect their children, and are diligent in looking after the affairs, generally, of their households, how many there are who do not come up to the full measure of their duty, especially in relation to their husbands. They seem to look upon their own interests, or those of the family, as being something separate from the interests of its head. Thus they consider whatever is added to the furniture or wardrobe as so much gained, without reflecting that every superfluous expenditure is a sum withdrawn from the general fund to which they must all look for support. And if their husbands become embarrassed in business, they regard these domestic acquisitions as a clear saving, forgetting that the money thus laid out may have been one of the causes of these embarrassments.

Nor should it be matter of surprise that this

is the case, since so many husbands do but little to make their wives feel their responsibility as partners—as sharers with them in all their concerns. It is this want of entire community of feeling in regard to all their interests which gives rise to the error so common among married women—that of regarding the prosperity of their families as an object of higher importance than the commercial or political integrity of their husbands. But the honour of her husband should be as dear to a wife as her own honour; and to sustain it, she should be willing to submit to every sacrifice of ease or comfort. If she is not always ready, however, to do this, and the privations anticipated from her husband's failure in business or his loss of place sometimes more deeply affect her than the disgrace that would attach to his name from acting unfaithfully or dishonestly, the blame is rarely altogether hers. It is the duty of man towards the woman he has chosen for his partner through life, to make her feel an equal interest with himself in the preservation of his honour, and in the prudent and successful management of his affairs. Nothing will more powerfully tend to elevate the character of his wife, and promote his own prosperity in life. A woman who has learned the value of money, its judicious and economical disbursement, and the prices she should pay for articles necessary for her household, is far more capable of managing the expenses of her family than her husband, from his ignorance of domestic economy, can possibly be. It is a well-known fact, that when the husband is the provider for the table, there is generally, if not always, a greater quantity purchased than is needed, and usually at higher prices. And even in articles of furniture or clothing, a man is liable to the same excess of expenditure, from his ignorance as to what is requisite or sufficient. A judicious female economist can furnish her house with taste, and provide for the daily wants of her table far better and cheaper than her husband. Men are losers in every way by not charging their wives with the responsibility of managing the family expenditures, and by keeping them ignorant of the limits within which they must be confined. Though a man in business should not be disposed to acquaint his wife fully with the state of his affairs, yet, in justice to himself and his family, he should make known to her the yearly sum he can afford to appropriate to the expenses of his household; and, after doing this, he should intrust it to her that they do not live beyond it. By confiding the expenditure of this amount to the judgment of his wife, he will avoid the unnecessary outlay he would be so likely to make himself, and prevent extravagance in her; for it is doubtless true, that female extravagance is more frequently owing to ignorance of the husband's income, and not being led to take a proper interest in his pecuniary concerns, than to any other cause. In thus depriving woman of her just share of responsibility in matters which equally affect their common welfare, man is the first transgressor, and usually, as he deserves to be, the greatest sufferer.

To the unreflecting these things may appear to be of trifling importance in cultivating moral greatness in woman; but it is the want of responsibility which has made so many of our females of the present day so inefficient, dependant, and useless in the domestic relation. Place them in any situation which will compel them to *think* and *act* for themselves, whether it be to have the immediate care and instruction of their children, the management of their domestic concerns, or the regulated expenditure of a portion of their husband's income, and the responsibility thus incurred will almost necessarily lead to strength of purpose and energy of character. Contrast the character of a virtuous woman, as drawn by Solomon, with that of our women of the present day, and it will be seen, notwithstanding our boasted advance in civilization, how far they come short of his standard. "Her price," he declares, "is far above rubies"—"She looketh well to the ways of her household, and eateth not the bread of idleness"—"She stretcheth out her hand to the poor; yea, she reacheth forth her hand to the needy"—"The heart of her husband doth safely trust in her, so that he shall have no need of spoil. She considereth a field, and buyeth it with the fruit of her hands; she planteth a vineyard. She maketh fine linen and selleth it, and delivereth girdles unto the merchant. She is like the merchant's ships: she bringeth her food from afar; she perceiveth that her merchandise is good. *Strength* and *honour* are her clothing. She openeth her mouth with wisdom, and in her tongue is the law of kindness." Thus, without passing beyond the limits of her proper sphere, she is represented as discharging all the duties of charity and of kindness; as exhibiting the highest qualities of a noble mind; and even as assisting to provide for the support of her household, as well as looking diligently to "its ways." And a woman like this, combining wisdom and love with so much trustworthiness, strength, and energy of character, he describes as finding her most grateful reward in her children rising up and calling her blessed, and in the praises of her husband. The wisest of men adds, " Give her of the fruit of her hands, and let her own works praise her in the gates;" therein laying down a rule of justice in regard to woman's rights over her own property far more correct than any recognised by our modern laws.

" The moral independence of woman," says a late writer in the Westminster Review, " has not yet taken its proper place as a principle in female education. Self-respect and self-reliance should be cultivated." Mrs. Jameson also observes, that " in woman, as now educated, there is a want of cheerful self-dependance;" and in its place, " a cherished physical delicacy and weakness of temperament, falsely deemed, in deference to the pride of man, essential to feminine grace and refinement." A very slight notice of what is passing around us will convince any reflecting mind of the truth of these remarks. No one who has studied the aggregate character of our youthful females but must have noticed their helpless dependance, their want of moral strength, and their deficiency in physical energy. These have arisen from the perversion of the qualities inherent in woman's nature, from the wrong principles adopted in her education, and from the false models presented for her admiration by novelists and poets, and sanctioned by society; such models having been drawn, not for the best good of the sex or of the human family, but solely for the gratification of the self-love and pride of man. Even Coleridge, the philosopher as well as poet, is said to have declared, that "the perfection of woman's character is to be characterless." And again he asserts, that "every man would like to have an Ophelia or a Desdemona for his wife." Mrs. Jameson, in noticing these remarks, adds, "No doubt! The sentiment is truly a *masculine* one." Were we to judge man's sentiments by the pictures he has so often drawn of woman, we might agree with her in this conclusion. But, though in his idle, dreaming hours, he may have sketched woman as he would have her for his mere amusement and pastime, yet in his better moments of reason and reflection he would cast from him such a being as a useless burden, and turn to the woman of intelligence and character as alone suited to be his companion for the serious purposes of life. He would then scorn the feeble, helpless creature his pencil had drawn, and despise her for the very characterlessness he had assumed to be her perfection.

The assertion that it is woman's perfection to be characterless is as false in fact as it is in the philosophy of human nature. An opinion like this may suit the pages of fiction, or it may please man in the hours of courtship to have his imagination beguiled with such a vision of the woman he loves. He may delight to picture her as worshipping him with a blind idolatry, looking up to him as a being perfect and infallible, leaning upon him in utter helplessness and with clinging dependance, thinking only as he thinks, feeling only as he feels, without exercising a single faculty of thought or action independent of his approval or direction. All this may be very gratifying to his vanity and his self-love; but when the fond worshipper becomes the wedded wife, these hues of fancy quickly give place to the sober colours of truth. She may be all he has imagined her to be; yet, if he find her incompetent to her duties as the mistress of his household and the mother of his children, unable to act or think without incessantly wearying him with petitions for assistance or advice, he will turn away disappointed and dissatisfied from one so wholly unprepared for the realities of life.

By men of less selfishness the ideal woman may be viewed in a different light, but one equally false and delusive. With these, the loved one is to be the idol, and they the worshippers. They elevate her to the pedestal, and bow down before her. They look upon woman as a being formed to sooth and amuse them in their leisure, but too delicate and too precious to be subjected to the slightest hardship or toil. This, too, is all delusion; and if men unconsciously err in supposing such to be the appropriate character and true position of woman, their mistake will result in bitter disappointment; or, if in this they intentionally deceive woman, and thus prevent her from attaining the intellectual and moral elevation of which she is capable, then their hypocrisy will be visited with its just reward, in finding their inefficient and characterless wives the greatest drawback to their own elevation, and the most fertile source of their unhappiness. It is painful to reflect how many lovely beings are led fatally wrong by these flattering and deceptive pictures: they listen with enchantment to fictions which so well accord with their indolent feelings, and with the round of trifling vanities

T

in which they pass their days, and sooth their imaginations with the expectation of a married life of luxurious ease and uninterrupted leisure—with fond, idolizing husbands, who will gratify their every whim; who will be blind to all their faults, and exaggerate all their virtues; and ransack earth and sea to lay each shining gewgaw at their feet. They experience a delightful complacence in viewing their own images thus reflected in the flattering mirror held up before them, and fancy themselves to be perfect models of what man wishes woman to be. They are as willing to be thought angels as they will be ready to claim the privilege of angels—that of having nothing to do with the labour expected from beings of earthly mould. But let them once become wives, and they will discover how much they have been deluded by their own imaginings, and by the false views presented of their sex; and find, after all, that man expects them to be something more than an idol or a toy. The lover, in his days of courtship, may amuse himself and sooth his affianced with flattery instead of teaching her truth; but when he comes to be a husband, he will tell her that, however well the idle visions of romance may be suited to girlhood, the sober duties of reality are expected from the wife

And were she now to remind him of his once uttered sentiments, he would only laugh at her folly in having supposed him serious; or, perhaps, even reproach her, as has sometimes been the case, for the very qualities he formerly pretended so much to admire.

Man often acts with so much irrationality in entering upon the married state, that were he to exhibit the same conduct in any other action of life, he would almost be deemed unsound in mind. "Trifles light as air" attract his eye and captivate his heart. He pursues the pretty flutterer from flower to flower until he has secured his prize, and then, for a while, takes pleasure in gazing upon his bright captive, and gratifies his vanity by exhibiting it to others. Of this, however, he soon grows weary, and begins to look for something more intrinsically valuable than mere external beauty. But he has caught his butterfly, and why should he expect from it the qualities of the provident, industrious bee? He must make the best of the choice he has made, and regard his disappointment as but the just reward of his folly. He cannot even claim commiseration: this is due only to the object of his delusion—to the helpless being he has enticed from a home of luxurious ease and a life of indolent gayety, to take upon herself the most serious duties, without the smallest previous instruction as to their nature, or qualification for their fulfilment.

Life at every season has its appropriate duties; and though parental indulgence may unwisely neglect to exact from an unmarried daughter those incumbent on her, still, when she enters a husband's home, she will not be the less required to meet the responsibilities connected with it. Indulgent as her husband may be, he most probably cannot, if he would, exonerate her from all effort and care, as her parents have done. Her situation has been greatly changed; and she will now find herself in a position where responsibility is forced upon her, and where she needs, every day and every hour, that self-reliance which she has been so little taught in her girlhood. To be "characterless," she will now bitterly experience, is to be wholly unfitted for the duties of a wife, a mother, or the mistress of a household. Away, then, with such preposterous fallacies. Married or unmarried, woman must have character —strong-minded, energetic character—to prepare her for the trials, the vicissitudes, and the responsibilities of life. The feeble, helpless thing that sentimental poets and visionaries would make her, might suit the climes where she is immured in a harem, amused with confectionary and bawbles, and decorated with fine clothes and jewels, to be the toy of some ignorant, animalized tyrant; but woman, in our enlightened and Christian land, is expected to be the intelligent, efficient helpmate of man. Let the models, then, that are presented for her imitation be such as correspond with her high destination; such as the philosophic Wordsworth eloquently portrays in the following lines:

> And now I see, with eye serene,
> The very pulse of the machine:
> A being breathing thoughtful breath,
> A traveller 'twixt life and death,
> The reason firm, the temperate will,
> Endurance, foresight, strength, and skill—
> A perfect woman—nobly plann'd
> To warn, to comfort, and command;
> And yet a spirit still and bright,
> With something of an angel's light.

One reason, doubtless, why some men are so much pleased with seeing the woman of their choice a creature full of softness, dependance, and engaging weakness, is, that they imagine amiability and gentleness are only to be found in such. But it requires very little knowledge of human nature, or experience in life, to discover that insipidity is not gentleness, nor characterlessness any warrant for amiability. Calm, forbearing gentleness, and a meek, quiet spirit, are seldom found in the feeble-minded, passive, and unreflecting. The women, again, who have been described as " fine by defect, and beautifully weak," are incapable of deep, enduring affection; for this beautiful weakness enters as well into the emotions of the heart as the operations of the mind. To love deeply, truly, and devotedly, through joy and sorrow, in adversity and in separation, from girlhood to womanhood, and from womanhood to declining age, woman must possess a force of character corresponding with this strength and durability of affection. She whose countenance ever wears the same unmeaning and picture-like aspect, unchanged by any emotion, and whose temperament is like the frozen lake, reflecting neither the blue sky, the cheerful sunshine, nor the passing cloud, cannot be a fitting companion for a man of sensibility or intellect. Mere animal tranquillity is not amiability, for true amiability is spiritual loveliness—the graces of the mind and heart exhibited in action.

Man may also be induced to depress woman into a state of helpless dependance, the more effectually to maintain his lordly sway. Christianity and civilization have broken the fetters which bound her as his slave, and to secure his remaining authority he may consider it politic to keep her feeble in mind and character. But, if this is sometimes the case, the plan is but poorly calculated to effect the proposed end. The wives who govern their husbands are for the most part women of weak intellect, capricious temper, and possessing that management and cunning resorted to by the feebler animals to make amends for their want of physical strength. But a woman of mind, feeling, and judgment scorns everything wearing the semblance of contrivance, artifice, or deception. Such a woman will never be found practising hypocrisy, or seeking " to rule by *seeming* to obey ;" for in her eyes all seeming is utterly inconsistent with that simple frankness and dignified integrity which should mark the conduct of woman. She has no desire to rule where she feels it to be her duty, as it is her highest pleasure, to " love, honour, and obey ;" and she submits with cheerful acquiescence to that order in the conjugal relation which God and nature have established. Men, therefore, greatly err in their jealousy of elevated, energetic, intellectual women. It is not these who are dangerous to their just prerogatives, but women without strength of character—the ignorant, the whimsical, the weak-minded, and the artful. It is such who bind the Gulliver with innumerable chains, seemingly weak when taken separately, but the united strength of which holds him in helpless bondage. Thus man is in every way a loser by depressing the character of woman instead of seeking to elevate it; and Taylor, in his "Natural History of Society," makes this very just remark: "Wherever woman is degraded by the pride or passion of man, from her proper position as a help meet for him, to his toy, his slave, or his victim, she has avenged herself by acquiring illegitimate influence as a compensation for her rights; and female power is generally most formidable where it is least recognised." But if the fallacious teachings of man, prompted by selfishness and pride, are thus visited back upon him, how deeply injurious are they to woman. Happily, however, experience, that stern teacher of truth, generally convinces her of their falsehood before she is wholly shorn of her strength. She is brought to feel the necessity of a self-supported energy, and that to be feeble, helpless, and dependant is to be entirely unfitted for all the real purposes and business of life. While she is under the parental roof, with no care, and her most trifling wants supplied, she may be unconscious of this truth; but no sooner is she placed in a situation where the obligations of a wife and a mother rest upon her, than it is revealed to her in all its force. Or should she be deprived of parental support and protection by the hand of death, how keenly, in her orphanage, will the consciousness of her deficiencies be felt. Even though she be left with a competence, she will still have need of self-reliance; but if the blight of poverty be added to the desolateness of her condition, how bitterly then is the conviction forced upon her, that her only earthly dependance is upon her own strength. Still, it is a salutary, though a painful lesson. Many a female, spoiled by parental indulgence, has been strengthened into mental vigour and moral greatness by the keen air of adversity.

I have seen such cases—an only child, for instance—the petted darling of her doting father, by whom her every whim was gratified, and who was permitted to indulge in every childish vanity or amusement without a thought or a care for the future. Her gayety gave such gladness to his heart that he could not consent to have it repressed by anything of a more serious nature. Thus her intellectual and moral culture was sadly neglected. The fond father died, and left his darling the heiress of a large fortune—but to the guardianship of strangers;

for he had no kindred to whom in her helplessness he could commit her. As she was known to be thoughtless and giddy, and had given no evidence of strength of character, it was predicted she would fall an easy prey to some fashionable fortune-hunter. But, child as she was, she soon learned the necessity of thinking and acting for herself. She appreciated the difficulties and the duties of her situation as an heiress and an orphan, and prepared herself to meet them. To the surprise of her acquaintance, she rapidly attained a strength of character and intellect far beyond her years, and this protected her against the numerous suiters who sought to win her merely for her wealth. Such was the knowledge of business she acquired, that before she was of age she was fully competent to manage her estate. When the time of her guardianship expired, she made an exact estimate of her income, with the view of appropriating it to useful purposes. Reserving but an inconsiderable portion for her own personal expenses, so small as to require of her the utmost prudence and economy in its expenditure, she applied the residue to works of charity—to the education of the orphan, and to the relief of the poor and afflicted. The principles of religion, which had taken deep root in her heart, grew with her growth and strengthened with her strength, imparting wisdom to her mind, and manifesting themselves in all her conduct. She looked to God for his blessing on her endeavours, trusting in his goodness, and relying upon his promises. Thus the giddy, petted child became intellectually and morally great in her maturity—a woman universally admired, respected, and honoured by all who knew her.

Again, I have known another—a fair and gentle creature, timid as the fawn, and tremblingly alive to everything like trial or danger—the idol of her fond parents, gratified in every wish, and flattered and caressed by all her acquaintance. She was of rare beauty; delicate and lovely as the " lily of the valley," spring's fairest, purest flower. She appeared a being formed to be cherished under the gentlest influences of love and happiness; and her shrinking sensitiveness and keen susceptibility were so agonizingly wrought upon by the sight or endurance of the slightest sorrow or suffering, that it seemed as though the afflictions of life, common to all, must prove fatal to her existence. But how different from this did she prove herself in the hour of trial. The first heavy grief that fell upon her was the death-sickness of her dear father. When the dreadful tidings were communicated to her that he could not live, instead of abandoning herself to despair, she calmly took her place beside his bed and never left it. With almost superhuman fortitude in one so young and so acutely susceptible, she ministered to him night and day, refusing rest and sustenance, and devoting every moment to the vain effort to alleviate the pangs of her dying parent.

Death came; and the gentle, lovely child was left not only fatherless, but portionless. When the sorrowing mother found that, with her departed companion, she had lost all means of support for her family, she sank into helpless despondency. She had always been accustomed to lean with entire dependance upon her husband, to look to him for advice and assistance in every difficulty, and had no strength to encounter adversity. But not so with her daughter. She who had been nurtured in luxurious ease, with the expectation of uninterrupted happiness, buried her grief in her stricken heart, calmly surveyed their situation, and resolutely prepared to meet its responsibilities. She saw the necessity of exertion, and made every effort, though in vain, to rouse her mother from the benumbing effects of her bereavement: she had too long indulged the helplessness of dependance to be invigorated by adversity. But affliction had wrought its perfect work upon the youthful daughter; a mighty change had come over her; the dormant energies of her character were fully roused into action. At the death-bed of her father she had learned a lesson of moral greatness that had made a deep and indelible impression upon her heart. She became a "wonder unto many;" and as she passed through her bitter trials with calm Christian fortitude, and the tranquil dignity of a mind prepared for every conflict, all who saw her felt that she possessed a self-sustaining power that was truly admirable.

To one who spoke of her youthfulness, she replied, with a sweet though melancholy smile, "Yes, I am young in years, but old in heart." In her, adversity had, indeed, anticipated the effects of many years' experience; and, were it permitted to intrude upon the sacred privacy of domestic life, a name might be given as worthy of honourable mention as any that have adorned the pages of the biographer; and the record of her life would present a striking instance of moral greatness.

To acquire firmness of mind and energy of purpose is to man comparatively an easy task:

these are in accordance with the distinctive traits of his character; and one of the first lessons he learns is to appreciate the power of his own free will. With him there is no unequal struggle between physical weakness and mental vigour—between the sensitiveness that instinctively shrinks from difficulty, and moral courage. He alone, from the inherent qualities of his nature, can proudly resolve "to still bear up, and steer right onward." But woman's power of endurance must, in due dependance on God, be derived from self-culture; and she can attain the same energy of will and action only by great self-denial and the most determined efforts. It is in her nature to be dependant. With her, from infancy to womanhood, there is an instinctive tendency to look up to the strong mind for counsel and guidance, and to lean upon the strong arm for protection and support. She experiences, indeed, a soothing, tranquil pleasure in this very feeling of dependance, which too often, alas! leads her to commit her all of faith, and hope, and love to some one unworthy of the trust. The love of sway and the desire for rule, with which she is so often taunted by those who are incapable of knowing or appreciating her, have no foundation in fact, and are libels on the sex. Woman feels she is not made for command, and finds her truest happiness in submitting to those who wield a rightful sceptre in justice, mercy, and love. From this principle of her nature it is that she is so susceptible of religious impressions, and so readily yields the homage of her heart and affections to Him on whom she can repose all her cares and hopes.

Natural force of character does not belong to woman; and although we sometimes find a female, seemingly by her native energies, bearing up under trials and difficulties with masculine firmness and resolution, yet there are moments when even she will feel as deeply her need of support as the feeblest of her sex. She may appear to the world as fully capable of sustaining herself, unaided and alone; but in her inmost heart she feels she is a woman still. Relying solely upon the strength derived from the power of her own will, she has no security for a *continued* capability of endurance. Without moral strength derived from self-culture, she will, at times, be feeble and vacillating. It is only by the discipline of thorough and efficient self-training, and the establishment of fixed principles, that she can arrive at true moral greatness. The gift of genius can do as little as her natural energies in fortifying the heart of woman. It may, indeed, by some be deemed a tower of strength, and the fame it brings sufficient to satisfy her utmost wishes; but let her speak from the depths of her spirit, and what will she tell us?

> "Fame, fame! thou canst not be the stay
>   Unto the drooping reed,
> The cool, fresh fountain in the day
>   Of the soul's feverish need.
> Where must the lone one turn or flee?
> Not unto thee, oh! not to thee."

However self-supported the brilliantly gifted woman may appear to the world, or amid the crowd of fashion's heartless triflers, in her hours of thought and seclusion her nature yearns for a home of rest, in dependance on some kindred heart. How strikingly do the histories of two of England's most talented daughters reveal to us woman's sympathies, and how impressively do they indicate the only unfailing source of her strength. In Mrs. Hemans and Miss Landon we see that genius, though it may give unbounded power over the hearts of others, gives not its possessor the same power over her own.

In the early years of Mrs. Hemans we discover a disposition to hero-worship—woman's feebleness putting forth its tendrils to seek support from another's strength. At length she met with one uniting in himself, as she fondly imagined, every perfection, and wedded the paragon she had long mentally idolized. She had endowed him with every spiritual and intellectual excellence that her genius could create, but, alas! it was her lot to give

> Sumless riches from affection's deep—
> To make an idol—and to find it clay.

How touching are the revelations of her heart's sufferings, unconsciously made known to us in her poetic effusions. In her wildest romancings we detect the sad reality, and in the lightest, gayest strains of her muse are heard the sighs of a broken spirit. Her affections had been cast to the earth, but she gathered them up and garnered them in the depths of her stricken heart. Taking her infant children by the hand, she sought out for them a home of her own, to which her husband never came. To provide for these helpless little ones, she was forced, though with an aching brain and a weary spirit, to sketch the bright visions in which she had dreamed away her life, and to indite, for bread, the high and glorious thoughts which had so often stirred the depths of her soul. The harrassing trials of life, and her every-day encounter with the mercenary and the heartless, wearied and sickened her, and she felt herself a stranger and a pilgrim on the earth. Her genius, brilliant as it was, imparted to her no moral strength, and merely brought to her an occasional and transient oblivion of her woes. She passed onward in her journey, unobservant even of the few green spots that are to be found in the most rugged pathway, while clouds of doubt and distrust concealed from her the bright heaven above. But as the light of Divine Truth gradually broke in upon her soul and dispelled these clouds, she felt more and more that God had been merciful to her in all his chastenings. And as her faith grew stronger, and her spirit became elevated and invigorated by her conflict with adversity and sorrow, she found the " mystery of her life solved." It was then that she received strength and consolation from above; and, no longer giving utterance to the mournful complaints of a blighted heart, she struck her harp to seraphic strains. At her appointed time she was removed from earth, that her spirit and her strength might be made perfect in Heaven.

The circumstances in the early life of Miss Landon were widely different from those in Mrs. Hemans', and would appear to have been more favourable to the development of self-dependance. The childhood and a long period of the womanhood of Mrs. Hemans were passed in the parental home, where she was fondly cherished by a mother's love, blessed with the affections of sisterhood and brotherhood, and relieved from every responsibility and care. But Miss Landon was left "an orphan in her first years," and thus young was cast upon the ocean of life, without chart or pilot, to trace her unaided way. True, she says of herself,

> "I early learned
> To make my heart suffice itself, and seek
> Support and sympathy in its own depths."

But who that has read her character, as revealed in her writings, does not discover in it the feelings of dependance so instinctive in woman's nature, left to its own feebleness, without the strength derived from self-culture, or from the support she might have experienced from religious truth, had she sought for Divine aid humbly and prayerfully? We are told, indeed, by those who saw her in society as the gay, heedless follower of every idle pleasure, that her real character was not to be judged by the feelings and sentiments which she expressed as an authoress; but we should rather say that a single thought, seriously uttered by her in the hour of solitude, was more to be relied on as a test of character than all that could be seen of her amid the masquerade of the fashionable world. It has been said, also, that she was too independent of the world's opinion; but it might be more truly said that she complied too much with it. The erratic impulses of her genius may have sometimes led her, through a momentary thoughtlessness, to violate its conventional rules; but still, she gave far more heed to the world than to the truths revealed to her in her better moments. She gave herself up to its follies and its fashions, and became a "bright, particular star" among its bewildering lights—among them, but not of them; for she had wandered from her own high place, and how painfully conscious she was of this sad truth, let her own words express:

> "I live among the cold, the false,
>   And I must seem like them;
> And such I am; for I am false
>   As those I most condemn.
>
> I check my thoughts, like curbed steeds
>   That struggle with the rein;
> I bid my feelings sleep, like wrecks
>   In the unfathom'd main.
>
> Surely I was not born for this:
>   I feel a loftier mood
> Of generous impulse, high resolve,
>   Steal o'er my solitude.
>
> I gaze upon the thousand stars
>   That fill the midnight sky,
> And wish, so passionately wish,
>   A light like theirs on high.

* * * * * * * * *
A step, a word, a voice, a look—
  Alas! my dream is done.
And earth, and earth's debasing stain,
  Again is on my soul,
And I am but a nameless part
  Of a most worthless whole.

But one fear—withering ridicule—
  Is all that I can dread—
A sword hung by a single hair
  Forever o'er the head."

What a revelation is here made of the stirring impulses and high resolves of genius, urging its possessor to act a noble part, and of the crushing weight of servile dependance on the world, fastened on woman by the fetters of fashionable society, and which she has not the moral strength to throw off. The withering ridicule of the world! this is the sword suspended over woman's head by a single hair, and this the phantom to frighten her from her duty, as we terrify children by some hideous image to make them yield to our will; as though either the ridicule or the applause of the world had any concern with her true elevation. The opinion of the world! what is it? It admits of no definite explanation, for it is constantly changing, and is in no two places exactly alike. She, therefore, who has no other or more fixed will to follow, must be helplessly left to the influence of every circle into which she may chance to be thrown, whether it be good or evil. Strange it is that rational beings should suffer themselves to be led by a guide so fallible and uncertain, when, by cultivating internal strength of principle, they might always have something on which they could safely rely. It has been from a mistaken idea of thus guarding female purity that woman has been taught to study the opinion of the world instead of the will of God and the approval of her own conscience. Virtue is not a matter of conventional rules and of limits prescribed by man, but has its seat in the heart, its laws written on the mind, and the word of God is the only infallible standard by which these laws are to be interpreted. If virtue be implanted in the soul, the outward conduct will at all times be governed by its principles; for the pure in heart sedulously shun the least appearance of evil.

We have only to look upon society to be convinced of the error of making the opinion of others the only standard of feminine propriety; for if we consider the changes wrought in public opinion by fashionable customs, we shall perceive that the world's ideas of female purity are as vacillating as its own usages. At one time, too free an exposure of the person is censured as a violation of female propriety; while at another, to be modestly attired is deemed an unnecessary fastidiousness. If fashion sanction unblushing freedom of manners, or latitude in conversation, the true refinement of virtuous feeling is condemned as prudery. It is but a few years since that the waltz was almost universally decried, even among the fashionable; and now it would create surprise to hear it reprobated, though it may be justly regarded as fatal to whatever is pure, and sacred, and lovely in woman. So shifting and inconsistent is the opinion of the world: why, then, should this poor, pitiful changeling be held up as a guide to woman? Both the world and its opinions are for the most part opposed to the Divine law; for the Word of Truth declares that "the carnal mind is enmity against God; is not subject to the law of God; neither, indeed, can be." But the laws of righteousness and truth are as immutable as the Omniscient One by whom they were established, and are alone worthy to direct a being destined for immortality.

What must be the enslaving power of the world's opinion over the feeble-minded and the frivolous, when we see one, whose spirit was stirred by high aspirations, and could give utterance to feelings like these—

> I have such eagerness of hope
> To benefit my kind,
> And feel as if immortal power
> Were given to my mind—

succumbing to its bondage, and selling her heaven-derived birthright of genius for its mess of pottage!

If it be woman's nature to be dependant, let her place her reliance upon that which is immutable in goodness and in truth, and not upon the unstable, erring world. Amid the heartless crowd of triflers by which she was surrounded, the affections of Miss Landon were as a hidden fountain, and there was no one to stir its depths; but no sooner did she meet one endowed with the mental pre-eminence she sought for, than she bowed before him an admiring worshipper. With woman's self-sacrificing devotion, she gave up all that had before been dear to her, to share with him a solitary home in a distant clime. She who had lived in the brilliant circles of fashion—the idol, and the "lion," of crowded saloons—cheerfully left the scene of her triumphs and the host of her flatterers, and immured herself in a lonely castle on the coast of Africa, where the voice of the melancholy sea, dashing against its base, was the only sound that met the ear, and with but a single companion to relieve the silence and monotony of her situation. And with what heartfelt alacrity did she enter upon these untried scenes, every anticipation brightened by hope, and every sacrifice lightened by love! How beautifully is woman's nature revealed in her letters, so full of affection and happiness—the first she wrote in wedded life; her resolutions to become all that a good housekeeper should be; her playful description of her mammoth bunch of keys, and of her pantry's stores: she, the brilliant child of fancy and of fashion, who had before scarcely given a thought to homely household cares, taking upon herself the busy, everyday duties of life with so much cheerfulness for the sake of him she loved! She loved as "woman genius only loves," and at his feet she laid all that had once strown pleasure in her path, choosing him for her only source of happiness, and surrendering up her liberty to make him the sole arbiter of her fate. Upon his truth and faithfulness she trustingly launched the bark freighted with her all of earthly hope and affection; but it struck upon a cruel rock, and was left a shattered wreck. Her dependance had been placed on mortality alone, and she had never been taught to look to heaven. In her hour of sudden trial there was no one to comfort her, and her heart fainted within her.

X

To have lived bereft of all that had been dear to her would have been to her a maniac's life. She shrunk with horror from the prospect of unceasing mental wretchedness, and, like Sappho on Leucate's rock, she stood for a brief moment on the brink of life's precipice, helpless and hopeless, and then, without one look into the fearful gulf of eternity, she threw herself into its abyss, and the dark waves closed over her.*

The history of Mrs. Hemans, so full of sad lamentations over blighted hopes, and the deep gloom which shrouds the fate of the gifted Miss Landon, are melancholy proofs that genius cannot give strength to bear up under the afflictions of life, or energy successfully to encounter its trials. And as we have seen that the instinctive dependance of woman makes self-reliance to her a difficult task, and that neither

---

* In speaking as we have of Mrs. Hemans and Miss Landon, the causes of their trials are, perhaps, more explicitly alluded to than is warranted by the studied silence of the English press respecting them. Yet there is a general impression produced by such testimony as has been given, and by the few obscure hints allowed to be whispered against living characters, which in some measure anticipates the verdict of the public; and from the distance of space which separates our country and England, we in many respects possess an advantage ordinarily enjoyed only by far-off distance in time—that of giving an opinion unbiased by prejudice or prepossession, by favour or fear.

talents nor genius can of themselves render her morally great, how forcibly does it show the necessity there is for a careful training of her powers of thought and action, and for self-exertion, on her part, in the exercise of those powers, that she may attain that moral strength of which she is constantly in need; for to be without this strength is to be in a great measure incapacitated for the discharge of her duties in every situation in life, and especially to encounter the vicissitudes and trials to which she is exposed. Even under the most favourable circumstances in which she can be placed, with an affectionate husband, who is unwearied in his attentions to promote the happiness and the welfare of their children, she will find that there is nothing which can compensate for a want of this power of self-reliance; that there will be occasions when she must act for herself, and cannot transfer her responsibilities to another, however great may be her incapacity.

Seeing, then, the importance of moral energy in the character of either sex, and that woman's nature instinctively leads her to look to another for protection and support, how unwise, irrational, and even cruel it is so to encourage and cherish this tendency as utterly to prevent the development of her nobler qualities. Her feelings of love and dependance, so beautifully harmonizing with her position in the social and domestic relations, were given her, not to impart feebleness to her character, but to soften and refine the rugged nature of man. All her endowments were intended for good, and should be made to answer the beneficent ends for which they were designed: her mind should be improved by judicious culture, her judgment strengthened by reflection, and her capacity for action fortified by energy and decision; and, when thus prepared for the trials and duties of life, let her be woman still—with a heart yearning for something to love, that shall be worthy of her affection, and where she may securely repose her confidence.

But if, even in the happiest and most prosperous wedded life, woman has need to exert her own strength of mind, and to rely upon her own powers of action, how much more deeply will this necessity be felt, when, as is, unhappily, too often the case, she is called to mourn over blighted hopes, and to feel the bitterness of ill-requited affection. If it be her lot to be treated with harshness where she expected tenderness; to be wronged by injustice and oppression where she looked for kindness and protection; to meet with neglect and indifference instead of attention and love, then the value of self-reliance will be fully revealed to her. Sustained by this, she will be enabled to bear up under all the ills of her condition, and to fulfil her obligations as a wife no less faithfully from a sense of duty than she would have done from the impulse of affection. Thus strengthened, trials and difficulties, that would otherwise be insupportable, will prove comparatively light; and, aided by Him who reneweth the strength of those who wait upon him, she will be enabled "to run and not be weary, to walk and not faint."

Let every woman feel it to be her highest duty, then, to strive after moral greatness of character, and let parents and husbands aid her to the utmost in this endeavour. Support and protection are not all that is required at their hands. It is incumbent on fathers and mothers fully to prepare their children for the future, that they may have capacity to perform the duties, and strength to endure the trials of life; and upon husbands, more especially, rests the responsibility of elevating the character of their wives. "Husbands," says St. Paul, "love your wives, even as Christ also loved the Church, and gave himself for it—That he might present it to himself a glorious Church, not having spot, or wrinkle, or any such thing; but that it should be holy and without blemish." In the force of this comparison we see how great is the obligation resting upon husbands. But how seldom is the Scripture doctrine, as here solemnly stated, enforced by human teachers. While we have volume upon volume setting forth the duties of wives and mothers, how comparatively little is written or said in relation to those of husbands and fathers. We are constantly reminded of the influence of the wife over the husband, but is that of the husband over the wife less powerful for good or for evil? Or, rather, do not experience and observation ordinarily show that the character of the wife depends more upon that of the husband, than does the husband's upon that of the wife?

Man usually does not enter into the married state until after his character has become fixed, but woman most frequently in all the tender pliancy of youth, when so much may be done by kind attention and a training hand; and her love will stimulate her to exert her every power to the utmost to elevate herself to that standard of intellectual or moral excellence, which her husband is anxious she should attain.

Woman has, indeed, been most unjustly treat

ed, not in being withheld from place or power, whether social or political, but in being deprived of that rational culture to which she is entitled as an intellectual and morally responsible being. And strange it is that the study of human nature, in its original capacities and in its powers of action, should hitherto have had so little effect in correcting this wrong; that, notwithstanding all that has been written and read on the philosophy of mind, woman's training should still be conducted with so little wisdom.

We condemn the Chinese for barbarously crippling the feet of their women, while we, with scarcely more humanity, and with deeper injury, cripple in ours the growth of all that is vigorous in thought or energetic in action, by keeping them bound from infancy to maturity in habits of indolence, and of helpless dependance. We despise, again, the folly of the Turkish despot, who absurdly supposes that guards and imprisonment are required to keep woman virtuous, while we, instead of relying upon the cultivation of virtuous principles and of moral strength, adopt the scarcely less preposterous maxims of the world, which teach that woman's safety is in the social restrictions by which she is surrounded.

If to educate aright be so to improve the faculties of the young as to prepare them to take upon themselves the responsibilities belonging to moral and accountable beings—to enable them to act for themselves without a slavish dependance upon others, and with energy of spirit to work out their own moral elevation, then how miserably defective is the education which, under our present systems, is given to woman. She is trained up as though she were designed to be "under tutors and governors" the whole of her life—to be always a child. Nor, under these circumstances, can we deem it strange when we see so many around us who are women in growth, but children in character and in intellect. The physical nature expands in all its just proportions and to full maturity of form, while the intellectual and spiritual nature, that nobler, better part, is cramped and dwarfed into imbecility.

And woman has been wronged, too, in being upbraided for errors and weaknesses which are but the necessary result of her erroneous training. She has been represented as wanting the higher qualities of mind, and as being little more than a creature of instinct, because her instinctive tendencies have been nurtured into excess, while the education of her understanding has been sadly neglected. And if she has escaped the worst evils to which these errors would have doomed her, it is only because they have been averted by an overruling Providence, or counteracted by the conservative principles implanted in her nature. The mighty energies springing from woman's love—what have they not enabled her to accomplish? As the daughter, sister, wife, or mother, though feeble in herself, she has risen in the might of her affections, and wrought such deeds for those who were dear to her, as man in the fulness of his strength would not have dared attempt.

Were the intellectual faculties of woman strengthened by proper culture, there would be no occasion to reproach her with mental imbecility; and if industry, self-reliance, and energy were as carefully fostered as are indolence and helplessness, she would reveal a strength of character of which she is now deemed quite incapable. Were the principles of ingenuousness and simplicity implanted in her heart, in place of her being systematically trained in the *arts of seeming*, by which she is led to substitute appearance for reality, her words and actions would ever be regulated by sincerity and truth. Wherever confidence is generously reposed in her, and responsibility clearly and forcibly exhibited to her view, she learns to become worthy of that confidence, and faithful to an enlightened sense of duty. Is she capricious? it is because, from the faults of her education, she has no stable and fixed principles to regulate her judgment: or is she improvident? her improvidence is that of a child who has never been taught the value of money, and never been made to feel the importance of using it with prudence and economy. Her defects, therefore, should be ascribed to those who have neglected her proper training; nor is it just that she should be harshly rebuked for failings which she owes to the instrumentality of others.

But if those who are called upon by every consideration of affection and interest to strengthen and improve her faculties of thought and action, that she may be qualified for her appointed condition in life, neglect their duty, then let woman herself put forth her own strength, and task it to the utmost in acquiring that energy of character so indispensable to her usefulness and her happiness. Let every youthful female, as soon as she is old enough to appreciate her responsibilities and the great ends of her being, consider whether she is being trained to meet them. Does conscience admonish her of her incapacity? then let her at once commence the work of self-training; take note of her deficiencies, and strive to acquire the virtues and the habits of which she stands in need. Has she been nurtured in indolent helplessness? then let her learn to be active, diligent, and self-relying. If she has heretofore looked only to her own ease and gratification, she must now, in her youth, accustom herself to the cross of self-denial, that she may be the better enabled to bear it when she shall be called on to endure its heavier burden. If she has constantly leaned upon others for counsel, assistance, and support, let her remember that there may be a time when she will have to stand alone, with no human arm to sustain her, none to advise or aid her, or, perhaps, with no one even to feel for her or to love her. Then let her prepare herself for every event that may await her. Should her life be passed upon "the smooth surface of a summer sea," she will have lost nothing by being nerved to encounter the "lashing surge" and the "tempest's roar." Nay, from being fitted to meet the afflictions of life, she will be the better qualified to enjoy its peace and prosperity. But, should sorrow and adversity haplessly come upon her, then in the resources of her own spirit she will find an unfailing support, and be enabled to triumph over difficulties that would utterly prostrate the timid and helpless.

Nor is it for her own elevation only that every female should labour, but for that of her sex. Let those who have experienced the advantages of moral strength, and those who painfully feel their want of it, alike come forward in this noble work. If the customs of society tend to produce feebleness of character in the sex, let them strive to counteract it by their own efforts. Let woman everywhere be made conscious of her high responsibilities, and, in humble dependance on that strength which cometh from above, resolve to live up to them.

But it is religion alone that affords any sure foundation for moral greatness; and, resting on this, the feeblest may become strong.* In this, woman, in the early ages of the Church, found a might that enabled her to brave all the terrors of martyrdom rather than deny her Master and be an apostate from her faith; and in this alone will she find a power to sustain her now under the trials and conflicts of life. If she be but true to herself and faithful to her God, He will be her refuge and strength in every time of

* See page 257.

need. Trusting, therefore, in His goodness, and relying upon His promises, let her strive to improve to the utmost the capacities that have been given her, and she will not fail of attaining that moral elevation which properly belongs to her, and by which alone she can become, in the most exalted sense, a blessing and a helpmate to man.

Y

CONCLUSION.

In the foregoing pages the author has endeavoured to give a faithful representation of the moral and intellectual condition of woman in our beloved country. As an American female, she feels a deep interest in the well-being of American women. It has not been her object, therefore, to extol the virtues in which they excel, but to point out the faults which most loudly call for amendment. Believing that most of their deficiencies are to be ascribed to erroneous training and a want of proper self-culture, she has advocated the right of her sex to a thorough and efficient education, and urged upon them the necessity of working out their own elevation; for it is by these means alone that they can take the position in society which they were intended to occupy.

We have been complimented for our comparative superiority over the women of other nations, but in this we have no just cause for complacency. Let us look at our superior advantages, and consider what we might have been had we faithfully and fully improved them.

Respect is shown to woman in our country as a matter of *courtesy*, but have we sought to secure that higher deference which is spontaneously awarded as a *right* to those who truly deserve it? If we have been indulged in domestic ease and comfort, have our homes been improved as they should have been by our presence? Have we not too often given ourselves up to habits of indolence, or to the pursuit of vanity and folly? Let us faithfully examine ourselves, and we shall find that we are not what we should be. There is yet a great work to be wrought by us—a work which will require the strenuous exertion of all our powers. There are injurious influences operating within us, which are insidiously reducing us to a state of moral debility; and there are external causes found in our false systems of education, and in the luxurious habits of society, which are secretly undermining the strength of the female character. The family institution, our own fair inheritance, is in danger of being laid waste, while we are thoughtlessly wandering from its hallowed precincts. The influence of foreign customs, too, alien to our institutions, and hostile to our best interests, is proving fatal to our republican simplicity of character.

Home is our palladium, and our post of honour and of duty, and here we must begin the work of reform. It is in the family circle that the female character is best trained in early life, and female usefulness most beneficially exerted in maturity. Still we would not assign to the duties of any one prescribed and impassable limits. We seek only to make home obligations paramount to all others. With some, the faithful discharge of these requires comparatively but a small part of their time or attention; and we would have such actively engaged in every great and good work, whether of humanity or religion, so far as it can be done without sacrificing the domestic character of woman.

We would have American women to be morally great as well as practically useful; to be resolute, energetic, and self-denying, in pursuing the even tenour of their way amid all the trials and vicissitudes of life. But, above all, we would have them exalted by piety, the crowning grace of every virtue, and the source of all that is truly elevated in the female character.

Since the preceding sheets were written, the following affecting instance of moral and intellectual energy in humble life, recorded among the proceedings of the American Bible Society, has been published in the Northern Advocate. It is a plain statement of the difficulties encountered and overcome by a blind female in learning to read; and as the touching simplicity of the narrative would be lost by giving it in any other words than her own, a copy of her letter is subjoined.

"*To the Managers of the American Bible Society:*

"Highly esteemed friends, gentlemen, lovers of the Bible: As I cannot write myself, I have neither time nor talent to introduce this imperfect scrawl to your notice. I humbly ask you to receive it as a token of my love and gratitude to the *Lord* and *yourselves*. As he has made you the honoured instruments of endearing life to me, I know not by what means I could show my gratitude better, than to give you a simple detail of the course I have pursued to obtain the invaluable privilege of reading the precious Word of Life. At four months old the smallpox deprived me of my natural sight, and I had lived in the world until I had entered the forty-seventh year of my age when I received your generous present. This, gentlemen, endears life to me. It will not be *three years* until next July since I received your invaluable present. On the eighteenth of the month above named I commenced with the alphabet. That I learned the first day, two hours of which I spent in ascertaining the difference between the letters C and G; this I knew must be done while I had them in alphabetical arrangement. Then I proceeded to *feel* and *spell* the *Lord's Prayer;* and though I had not *five* hours' attention in *teaching* during the period of three weeks, yet, notwithstanding, from intense study I accomplished the same. I then took the Scriptural sheet which contained a part of the 22d and 23d chapters of Acts: I felt, spelled, and read them in *three* weeks more. After six weeks had elapsed, I found, from loss of *sleep* and *appetite*, I was becoming much debilitated; my hands were affected with tremours, which rendered it quite difficult for me to trace the lines with my fingers. I then found I could not accomplish this grand and important enterprise without the benefit of instruction. *Now*, thought I, *what shall I do?* I am *poor*, and cannot employ an instructer. My next effort was to gain admittance into the institute for the benefit of the blind. I obtained a recommendation from the board of freeholders in the county of my residence, and presented it in person to the board of managers. They observed that my *age* was against my entrance; but as I only desired to learn to read the plain Scriptures, if I could obtain a formal order from the governor of the State of New-Jersey, they would then admit me into said institution for the term of six months. When Mr. Toy, of Camden, N. J., understood *this*, he proceeded to the chief magistrate, at his own expense, and presented my case to him. The governor said the funds that had been placed into the treasury for that purpose were now exhausted; but if the Legislature should replenish the same, he then would grant me an order for entrance. But I felt that I had no time to lose, for I had then passed the age of forty-seven. For years I had been accustomed to take my *Bible* into a private room; there I *talked* to it, and *wept* and *prayed* over it; and as I did not succeed in this effort, I sat down by a friend, who wrote for me, and composed some poetry. I commenced my poem with my loss of sight in early infancy, and my early conversion to the Lord; then I put in verse my love for and talk to the Bible; then I borrowed money from a gentleman in Philadelphia to pay for the printing of my poem, and walked through the streets and courts of that city, and offered the same for sale to passers by for six cents each. I sold and disposed of a great number of them in the different class of rooms. Perhaps the quantity I sold in all were about 1200 in that city and New-Jersey, the proceeds of which I applied to the benefit of my instruction. I obtained a month and a half instruction for the sum of seventeen dollars. The want of health obliged me at this time to abandon my study. My limited circumstances in life had always obliged me to do something for my own support; my industry hardened my fingers, so as to require a heavy pressure of the hand to make the finger susceptible of the formation of the different letters; consequently, my fingers have been so cut off, as for the blood to follow them across many of the lines of my precious book; on one spelling lesson my friends counted thirty-six marks of blood from my worn fingers. I purchased the spelling-book from the institution in Philadelphia; I paid $2 50 for the same; also a volume of the Old Testament, including the books of Ruth and Esther; for that I paid $1 50. During my first month and a half instruction, I read and committed twenty-five verses of the first chapter of Christ's sermon on the mount. The next two months I read and committed from the fourth chapter of the same Gospel up to the eleventh; and since that period I have read regularly through the Testament to the twelfth chapter of Acts. I read each chapter three times before I leave it. I have paid for six months' schooling at ten dollars per month. I have enjoyed, strictly speaking, the benefit of five months' instruction; the other month I consider as being lost, on account of soreness of fingers and other unavoidable causes.

Now I believe I have given you a true, simple statement of all the particulars. I have told you of the course I have pursued in my own simple way, stating every circumstance as near as possible, and my reasons for so doing; first, to let you know that your labour of love is not lost; second, a hope inspires my heart to think that this simple statement will induce you to pity some other poor unfortunate creatures, and bestow upon them the same invaluable blessing. I am subscribed your humble debtor.

MARY S. COLLINS.
Leedsville, Atlantic co., N. J., May 12, 1841."

What an example of Christian energy and of moral strength is here presented to us! It was to be enabled to read her Bible that this poor, blind female submitted to all this self-denying exertion; and through poverty and physical suffering she persevered, until the Sacred Pages she had *talked to, wept and prayed over*, became legible to her mental eye. We may have sympathized with Newton in his overpowering emotion at the grand result of his mighty labours, but who can appreciate the feelings of this daughter of affliction on attaining the glorious object for which she had been struggling? And what a rebuke does her example administer to those who are blessed with sight, and with ample means for instruction, and yet neglect to apply them to the noblest of all purposes—the study of the Bible. The gift of sight and the ability to read—alas! how little do we appreciate our common blessings, and how much abuse them!

THE END.

www.ingramcontent.com/pod-product-compliance
Lightning Source LLC
Chambersburg PA
CBHW081324090426
42737CB00017B/3027